700 FACTS ABOUT AFRICA

Adesanya Ayeni

Edited by Mallami Habeeb
Publisher by Adesanya Ayeni

Contents

General Africa Facts

1) Africa is a vast continent, with 54 countries. Although some confuse the entire continent with being a single country.
2) Africa is the second-largest continent in the world. The largest being Asia, of course.
3) Africa is home to over 1 billion people – half of which are younger than 25.
4) More than 1500 languages are spoken across the continent.
5) Population: 1,415,045,928.
6) Land area: 30,370,000 km2 (11,730,000 square miles).
7) Most spoken languages in Africa are Arabic, English, Swahili, Amharic, French, Yoruba, Oromo, Hausa, Igbo and Zulu.
8) Islam and Christianity are the two most common religions in Africa.
9) The smallest country in Africa is the Seychelles, which is also an island.
10) Algeria is the largest country by area with 2,381,741 square kilometres. It's the 10th largest country in the world.
11) Time zones: From UTC-1 to UTC+4.

12) The origin of the name "Africa" is greatly disputed by scholars. Most believe it stems from words used by the Phoenicians, Greeks, and Romans. Important words include the Egyptian word Afru-ika, meaning "Motherland"; the Greek word aphrike, meaning "without cold"; and the Latin word aprica, meaning "sunny."

Interesting and Random Facts

13) Nigeria has seen the most twins born in the world. This has earned the country the nickname "The Land of Twins".

14) Eighteen people from Africa have been awarded a Nobel prize. They come from Algeria, Egypt, Ghana, Kenya, Nigeria and South Africa.

15) Plastic packaging and non-biodegradable polythene bags are 100% banned in Rwanda. They're not allowed in the country at all and all luggage are searched at the airport to make sure of this.

16) 90% of the world's malaria cases originate in Africa. Thankfully this is only a problem in certain areas, and there are plenty of safe African countries to visit.

17) One of the oldest universities in the world is in Timbuktu, Mali. By the 12th century Timbuktu was home to three universities. Over 25,000 students attended one of the Timbuktu universities in the 12th century.

18) The Second Congo War claimed over 5.4 million lives and is the deadliest worldwide conflict since World War II.

19) Almost 40% of adults in Africa are illiterate – two-thirds are women. Adult literacy rates are below 50% in Benin,

Burkina Faso, Chad, Ethiopia, Guinea, Mali, Niger, Senegal, Sierra Leone and The Gambia.

20) Over 25 million people are HIV-positive on the continent and over 17 million have died of the disease already.

21) Arabic is spoken by 170 million people on the continent, followed in popularity by English (130 million), Swahili (100), French (115), Berber (50), Hausa (50), Portuguese (20) and Spanish (10).

22) The Pharaonic civilization of ancient Egypt is one of the world's oldest and longest-lasting civilizations.

23) The northern most point in Africa is Ras ben Sakka in Tunisia. The most southerly point is Cape Agulhas in South Africa.

24) Rainfall variability is very high – from 0 mm/year in the Sahara to 9,500 mm/year near Mount Cameroon.

25) Neo-colonialism is a real threat with over 1 million Chinese citizens on the African continent. Angola alone has a population of over 350,000 Chinese.

26) Approximately 90% of all cases of malaria worldwide occur in Africa, accounting for 24% of all child deaths in sub-Saharan Africa.

27) All of Africa was colonized by foreign powers during the "scramble for Africa", except Ethiopia and Liberia.

28) Before colonial rule, Africa comprised up to 10,000 different states and autonomous groups with distinct languages and customs.

29) The famous singer Freddie Mercury was born in Zanzibar, a group of islands just off the coast of Tanzania.

30) Nigeria, with a 2013 estimated population of 174,507,539 is the most populous Black nation and the 7th most populated nation in the entire world, trailing after—from least to most—Pakistan, Brazil, Indonesia, USA, India and China (1.3bn).

31) Libreville, Gabon is one of the most expensive city in the world to live in. Tokyo is the most expensive city.

32) Nigeria, with 521 languages has the fourth-most in the world. This includes 510 living languages, two-second languages without native speakers and 9 extinct languages.

33) The Portuguese reached Nigeria in 1472. In 1880 the British began conquering Nigeria's south. The north was conquered by 1903.

34) Yoruba tribe in Nigeria and their bloodlines worldwide have the highest rate of twinning (having twins) in the world.

35) South Africa is 5 times the size of Japan and 3 times the size of Texas.

36) Nigeria has more Muslims than Saudi Arabia
37) The 2006 Census found Nigerians to be the highest educated ethnic or racial group in America.
38) Nigeria's population was just 16 million in 1911. It is projected to hit 444 million by 2050, surpassing the US and becoming the 4th largest in the world.
39) The population of Lagos today is about more than the total population of all Eastern states combined.
40) Benin Kingdom: The high quality and highly sophisticated bronze work of the Benin Kingdom dating as far back as the 13th century is a world wonder. Great works in iron, wood, ivory, and terra cotta products also highlight the empire's history.
41) Benin Kingdom: Lourenco Pinto, captain of a ship that carried missionaries to Warri in 1619, described Benin kingdom, 'Great Benin where the king resides is larger than Lisbon, all the streets run straight and as far as the eyes can see….'
42) Pretoria (SA's capital city) was founded in 1855 by Marthinus Pretorius. He named it after his father, Andries Pretorius.
43) French is spoken by more people in Africa than in France. And Portuguese is spoken by a larger number of people in Africa than in Portugal.

44) The largest annual Christian gathering in Africa is hosted by the Redeemed Christian Church of God and it is called the Holy Ghost Convention. This was in Nigeria.

45) Nigerian immigrants in the US are one of the most educated

46) Over 55% of Africa's labour force working in food production with vast areas of arable and pastoral lands supporting agricultural economies.

47) Africans are one of the biggest contributors to sculptural art.

48) Important climatic regions of agriculture in Africa include tropical wet, savannah, desert, Mediterranean, and highland.

49) Africa has 135 UNESCO World Heritage Sites scattered across the continent.

50) Sudan has more pyramids than Egypt (200+ pyramids). But the largest pyramid is actually found in Mexico!

51) Nigeria's movie industry, Nollywood, is technically bigger than Hollywood.

52) 100 million Africans have Facebook accounts.

53) The movie Blood Diamond, starring Leonardo Di Caprio, had many of its most dramatic scenes shot in Maputo, Mozambique.

54) The Western Cape of South Africa is home to the longest wine route in the world. Route 62 spans 850kms and boasts some superb wineries.

55) It's considered rude to decline an offering of meat at meals in Morocco – vegetarians may have a hard time with this.

56) There's an African beer brewed from bananas. This is widely made in East Africa and goes by various names in different countries.

57) In rural markets in the province of Limpopo, Mopane worms can be found being sold as food. These are high in protein and the locals love them as a smoky snack.

58) In countries like Morocco and Algeria, couscous is a popular dish served with meat and vegetables.

59) In Western Africa, it is common for people to grow and eat cassava, maize, millet and plantains.

60) People living in what is currently Swaziland were the world's first miners. In the late 1960s a hematite mine was found in the Ngwenya mountain range along with 300,000 artifacts and stone-made mining tools that were later dated to be 43,000 years old!

61) Egypt is the most popular tourist destination in Africa, attracting around 10 million visitors per year.

62) The oldest known mathematical object is the Lebombo bone, which was discovered in the Lebombo Mountains of Swaziland. It dates to approximately 35,000 B.C.

Natural Resources and Economy

63) Johannesburg is also known as 'The City of Gold'. This is because it was largely established when gold was discovered in the surrounding areas, and it became a mining town.
64) Ghana is the world's second-largest producer of cocoa.
65) Nearly half of all gold mined has come from Witwatersrand, South Africa.
66) China is Africa's top trade partner with Africa.

China's direct investment in Africa exceeds $50 billion.

67) The continent contains 30% of the planet's mineral resources.
68) Nigeria is fourth-largest oil exporter in the world, and Africa's biggest oil producer with about 2.2 million barrels produced every day. Top 10 oil producers in order of total exports: Nigeria, Algeria, Angola, Libya, Egypt, Sudan, Equatorial Guinea, Republic of Congo, Gabon, and South Africa.
69) Africa has approximately 30% of the earth's remaining mineral resources.
70) 90% of all platinum metals are mined Africa, and over 40% of the world's gold comes from here. The continent

is rich in natural resources, and this is how many countries make their money.

71) Africa is home to five of the world's top oil-producing countries, with an estimated 57 percent of Africa's export earnings from hydrocarbons.

72) Algeria, Angola, Cameroon, Chad, Republic of Congo, Egypt, Eritrea, Gabon, Ghana, Kenya, Libya, Nigeria, South Sudan, Sudan, Tunisia, and Mozambique are all rich in oil and gas.

73) Africa is a major producer of important metals and minerals.

74) Metals exported by African countries include uranium, used to produce nuclear energy; platinum, used in jewellery and industrial applications; nickel, used in stainless steel, magnets, coins, and rechargeable batteries; bauxite, the main aluminium ore; and cobalt, used in colour pigments.

75) Africa's two most profitable mineral resources are gold and diamonds.

76) South Africa accounts for almost half of Africa's gold production. Ghana, Guinea, Mali, and Tanzania are other major producers of gold.

77) Africa dominates the global diamond market. In 2008, the continent produced 55 percent of the world's diamonds.

78) The Driefontein Gold Mine outside of Johannesburg, South Africa, is one of the largest gold mines in the world. The mine is made up of eight shafts that reach depths of up to 3,352 meters (11,000 feet) underground. One of the shafts is in the process of being deepened to about 4,115 meters (13,500 feet), making it the deepest mine in the world.

79) Botswana, Angola, South Africa, the Democratic Republic of the Congo, and Namibia are Africa's largest producers of diamonds.

80) African countries export a lot of forest products, especially high-grade woods like mahogany and Okoume. These products bring in significant revenue.

81) Africa forestry products are mostly found in the countries of the Congo Basin—Cameroon, Central African Republic, Republic of the Congo, the Democratic Republic of the Congo, Gabon, and Equatorial Guinea—where there is a dense rain forest.

82) Proven oil reserves have grown by almost 150 percent, increasing from 53.4 billion barrels since 1980, to 130.3 billion barrels by the end of 2012.

83) Nigeria and South Africa make up almost half of Africa's GDP. Nigeria especially has a large population which makes it a viable place to invest. However, Nigeria is definitely a challenging place to operate. But ultimately,

the nation is too important to ignore. Nigeria and South Africa account for nearly 50% of the continent's GDP.

84) In central and western Africa, where forest cover is heaviest, the forest sector contributes more than 60 percent of GDP.

85) Forestry, the management of trees and other vegetation in forests is an important economic activity in Africa. On average, forest products account for 6 percent of Africa's gross domestic product (GDP), more than any other continent.

86) Zimbabwe has one of the world's highest inflation and unemployment rates.

87) Manufacturing, mining, and farming constitute the backbone of the Zimbabwean economy.

88) The richest country in Africa is Equatorial Guinea while the poorest is Zimbabwe.

89) China is Africa's top trade partner with Sino-African trade volumes now nearing $200 billion per year.

90) Africa is the world's poorest and most underdeveloped continent with a continental GDP that accounts for just 2.4% of global GDP.

91) China's direct investment in Africa exceeds $50 billion.

92) The Johannesburg Stock Exchange is the oldest existing and largest stock exchange in Africa.

93) In 2034, Africa is expected to have the world's largest working-age population of 1.1 billion.

94) Besides oil and gas, Africa is rich in precious minerals, forests and:

- **Diamonds**: found in Angola, Botswana, Central African Republic, and the Democratic Republic of Congo.
- **Gold**: found in Benin, Burkina Faso, Djibouti, Mali, South Africa, and Tanzania.
- **Nickel and Uranium:** found in Burundi.
- **Pozzolana:** found in Cape Verde.
- **Fish:** found in Comoros, Guinea-Bissau, Mauritius, Sao Tome and Principe, Senegal, and Seychelles.
- **Timber:** found in Liberia.
- **Titanium:** found in Gambia.
- **Graphite:** found in Madagascar.
- **Tobacco:** found in Malawi.
- **Iron Ore:** found in Mauritania.
- **Phosphates:** found in Western Sahara, Morocco.
- **Aluminium and Gas:** Found in Guinea, Mozambique.
- **Cooper:** found in Uganda, Zambia.

95) Agriculture employs two-thirds of the continent's working population and contributes 20 to 60 percent of every country's gross domestic product (GDP). GDP is the total value of goods and services produced in a country during one year.

96) Important crops to Africa's tropical wet regions include the plantain, pineapple, coffee, cocoa, and oil palms. (Oil from this palm tree is the primary cooking oil in Africa, as familiar as olive oil or corn oil in North America.)

97) Important savannah crops include the cassava (related to the potato), peanuts, peppers, okra, eggplant, cucumber, and watermelon. Savannah conditions occur in much of eastern and southern Africa

98) Africa's most important grain crops, millet and sorghum, are grown here.

99) Important desert crops include date palms and cotton. Desert conditions occur in northern Africa, especially in the Sahara and the Sahel.

100) Important crops in Africa Mediterranean climate include figs, olives, oranges, tomatoes, onions, and large vegetables, such as cabbage and cauliflower.

101) Highland crops include alfalfa, potatoes, and wheat. Highland conditions occur in the highest elevations of Africa, particularly in the Ethiopian Highlands

102) Africa's fishing industry provides income to more than 10 million people and has an annual export value of $2.7 billion. Africa has fisheries on all its marine coasts, as well as inland.

103) The Great Lakes and Nile River, for instance, support huge freshwater fisheries.

104) West Africa is one of the most economically important fishing zones in the world, producing 4.5 million tons of fish in 2000.

105) Namibia and South Africa are also major players in the marine fish market, exporting between 80 and 90 percent of their fish annually.

106) The Eastern African countries of Eritrea, Djibouti, Somalia, and Kenya have well-established fisheries in the Red Sea and the Indian Ocean. Small fish such as herring and sardines are the most common catch on the African coastline. However, larger fish, such as tuna, cod, hake, and haddock, are the most profitable.

107) Lake Victoria is the most productive freshwater fishery in the world, producing more than 500,000 tons of fish worth $600 million every year.

108) The Nile perch, a highly prized catch that can weigh more than 45 kilograms (100 pounds), and the Nile tilapia are Lake's Victoria's dominant commercial fish species.

Man-Made & Inventions

109) In Cape Town, there is a large nuclear power station built on a fault line. The last tremor was felt in 1809 and measured 6.5 on the Richter scale. Scientists aren't sure when the next one will happen.

110) The 365-day calendar is believed to have been invented by the Egyptians. This helped them predict the annual Nile flooding.

111) There's a bar built into a 6000-year-old baobab tree, located in South Africa. You can visit to enjoy a drink all through the year.

112) Africa is home to several engineering marvels. The Aswan Dam, a complex of two dams in Aswan, Egypt, captures the world's longest river, the Nile, in the world's third-largest reservoir, Lake Nasser.

113) Computer science engineer, Arthur Zang invented the Cardiopad, a game-changing medical device that could save millions of lives in rural Africa and beyond.

114) The Aswan High Dam produces more than 10 billion kilowatt-hours of electricity every year, enough power for about 15 percent of Egypt.

115) Some houses in Tunisia are made from fish bones. This is because the locals believe fish have supernatural powers and will protect against evil spirits.

116) The Cocoa House in Ibadan, Nigeria was once the tallest building in Africa. It was built in 1965

117) The Dufuna Canoe is the oldest boat to be discovered in Africa. It was found in 1987 by a herder of Fulani descent, a little way from the village of Dufuna located in the Fune Local Government Area, sharing borders with the Komadugu Gana River, in Yobe State, Nigeria. The boat is the third oldest known canoe in the world.

118) Cape Town's Castle of Good Hope is the oldest building in South Africa. It was built between 1666 and 1679 by the Dutch East India Company.

119) The ironing board is a product that's used possibly just as much as it's overlooked. In the late 19th century, it was improved upon by Sarah Boone, an African-American woman who was born a slave. One of the first black women in U.S. history to receive a patent.

120) Home Security System, Co-Invented by Mary Van Brittan Brown in 1966. Before security systems became a fixture in homes, an African-American nurse Mary Van Brittan Brown, devised an early security unit for her own home. She spent many nights at home alone in Queens, New York while her husband was away, and felt unsafe

with the high rates of crime in her neighbourhood. On top of that, police were unreliable and unresponsive. So she created a device that would help put her mind at ease.

121) The Three-Light Traffic Light System was invented by Garrett Morgan in 1923. With only elementary school education, black inventor (and son of a slave), Garrett Morgan came up with several significant inventions, including the improved sewing machine and the gas mask. One of Morgan's most influential inventions was the improved traffic light. Without his innovation, drivers across the nation would be directed by a two-light system.

122) Otis Boykin contributed to circuit improvements to pacemakers after losing his mother to heart failure — a contribution that has saved countless lives since. But this single improvement was among a long list of his great achievements. Boykin had 26 patents in his name

123) Did you ever enjoy water gun fights as a kid? Lonnie Johnson is the man that gave us the most famous water gun — the Super Soaker. Lonnie wasn't a toymaker, he was actually an Aerospace Engineer for NASA with a resume boasting a stint with the US Air Force, work on the Galileo Jupiter probe and Mars Observer project, and more than 40 patents.

124)Automatic Elevator Doors, Invented by Alexander Miles in 1887. The use of elevators in everyday life keeps people from committing to long and gruelling climbs up several flights of stairs. However, before the creation of elevator doors that close automatically, riding a lift was both complicated and risky.

125)Charles Drew was a physician, surgeon, and medical researcher who worked with a team at Red Cross on groundbreaking discoveries around blood transfusions. In World War II, he played a major role in developing the first large-scale blood banks and blood plasma programs.

126) Electret Microphone, Co-Invented by James E. West in 1964. Along with his German colleague Gerhard Sessler, West invented the foil electret microphone, which was considerably less expensive to produce than the typically used condenser microphones.

127)In 1989, Philip Emeagwali used 65,000 processes to invent the world's first super computer — able to perform 3.1 billion calculations per second. Emeagwali received the 1989 Gordon Bell Prize for an application of the CM-2 massively-parallel computer. The application used computational fluid dynamics for oil-reservoir modeling. He received a prize in "price/performance" category, with a performance figure of about 400 Mflops/$1M.

128) Development of Voice over IP was credited to Marian Rogers Croak. She created most of methods and features that both improved Voice over IP reliability and ushered in its nearly universal adoption.

129) Carbon Light Bulb Filament, Invented by Lewis Latimer in 1881. The light bulb itself was invented by Thomas Edison, but the innovation used to create longer-lasting light bulbs with a carbon filament came from African-American inventor Lewis Latimer. Latimer, the son of runaway slaves, began work in a patent law firm after serving in the military for the Union during the Civil War.

130) As a mathematician for the American Optical Company in Buffalo, N.Y., Jesse Ernest Wilkins perfected lens design for microscopes and ophthalmologic uses. His greatest contribution was the development of mathematical models to explain gamma radiation and his work on developing a shielding against gamma radiation.

131) Lisa Gelobter was integrally involved with the advent of Shockwave, a technology that formed the beginning of web animation. She also played a major role in the emergency of online video

132) One of the most famous black inventors ever is McCoy who was credited for 50 inventions over the span of his

career. In an effort to improve efficiency and eliminate the frequent stopping necessary for lubrication of trains, McCoy devised a method of automating the task. In 1872 he developed a "lubricating cup" that could automatically drip oil when and where needed — vital in avoiding sticking to the track.

133) Mary Beatrice Davidson Kenner and her sister Mildred patented many practical inventions. They didn't have technical education, but they were both exceptional at spotting ways to make peoples' lives better. Together, they invented the sanitary belt. Later, Mary invented the moisture-resistant pocket for the belt. While disabled from multiple sclerosis, Mary went on to invent the walker and the toilet-tissue holder.

134) 6th October Bridge in Egypt is the longest bridge in Africa. The Bridge in Cairo, Egypt even almost doubles the length of the former record holder, 20.5 km long compared to 11.8 km of Third Mainland Bridge of Lagos. As of 2020, The 6th October Bridge is officially the longest bridge in Africa.

135) The First Storey Building in Nigeria is located in Badagry, Lagos State. It attracts many visitors every year. The foundation of the building was laid in 1842 while the house was completed in 1845. The one-storey building

has its corrugated iron sheet roof overlooking the marina waterfront.

136) Allan MacLeod Cormack who invented CT scan was born and raised in South Africa.

Natural Environment

137)The Sahara Desert is currently larger than the entire United States. And it continues to grow each year!

138) Senegal has a pink lake called Lac Rose. The pink colour is caused by a type of bacteria, but the lake is completely safe to swim in.

139)The gemstone Tanzanite is only found in Tanzania. It was discovered in the 1800s by a Masai warrior and today it's seen as one of the most precious gems in the world.

140) 90% of all platinum metals are mined Africa, and over 40% of the world's gold comes from here. The continent is rich in natural resources, and this is how many countries make their money.

141)Africa is the world's second driest continent (after Australia).

142)Six of the driest places in the world are in Africa – Al'Kufrah, Libya, Aswan and Luxor in Egypt, Wadi Halfa in Sudan, Pelican Point in Namibia and Aoelef in Algeria.

143)Limited groundwater represents only 15% of the continent's total renewable water resources. New discoveries of groundwater reserves in large sedimentary basins in Libya, Algeria and Chad may slack Africa's growing thirst for the next few decades

144) There are 16 landlocked countries in African. These countries are Botswana, Burkina Faso, Burundi, Central African Republic, Chad, Ethiopia, Lesotho, Malawi, Mali, Niger, Rwanda, South Sudan, Swaziland, Uganda, Zambia, and Zimbabwe.

145) Inside the country of South Africa is a smaller, landlocked country called Lesotho.

146) Morocco in Africa and Spain in Europe have less than 9 miles of ocean between them – creating the two continents' shortest distance.

147) Africa is the most centrally-located continent on the planet. Both the equator and the Greenwich Meridian line cross it.

148) Namibia is made up of a lot of desert land, and the Sossusvlei Sand Dunes rank in the top for the highest in the world. Sandboarding is a lot of fun in this country.

149) The productivity of about 65% of the continent's agricultural lands has declined significantly with vast tracts of land have been degraded by erosion, poor land management practices, mining and pollution over the last 50 years.

150) Kenya shares Lake Victoria with Tanzania and Uganda.

151) The Fish River Canyon in Namibia is the second largest canyon in the world.

152) Mount Kenya national park and Lake Turkana National park are world heritage sites in Kenya.

153) Sahara desert covers 11 countries (large sections of Algeria, Chad, Egypt, Libya, Mali, Mauritania, Morocco, Niger, Western Sahara, Sudan and Tunisia).

154) Water scarcity impacts the lives of over 300 million Africans, of whom approximately 75% of Africans rely on groundwater as their primary source of drinking water.

155) The longest river in the world, the Nile, is located in Egypt, Africa.

156) The world's largest desert (Sahara) is also situated in Africa.

157) Africa is the world's hottest continent, with a town in Ethiopia seeing average temperatures of 33.9 °C throughout the year.

158) The continent has the largest reserves of precious metals with over 40% of the gold reserves, over 60% of the cobalt, and 90% of the platinum reserves.

159) It's also the world's oldest populated continent.

160) Africa holds the name of being the biggest oil producer in the world.

161) The highest mountain on the continent is Mount Kilimanjaro.

162) Africa's largest island is Madagascar.

163) Africa's deforestation rates are double those of the rest of the world.

164) There are a total of 3000 protected areas in Africa. These keep the fauna and flora safe and living naturally in their habitats.

165) Africa is the world's second-largest continent covering about over 30 million square kilometres.

166) Shipwreck Point in Liberia is a mecca for globe trotting surfers. They come for the 10 metre waves between March and October.

167) Al'Aziziyah in Libya set the record of being the hottest place on Earth. Temperature of 57.8 ° C was recorded back on September 13, 1922.

168) Africa emits only 4% of total carbon dioxide emissions, which is impressive for such a large continent.

169) Africa is the world's hottest continent with deserts and drylands covering 60% of land surface area (e.g. Kalahari, Sahara and Namib).

170) Cape Town has the 5th best blue sky in the world (according to the UK's National Physical Laboratory).

171) The largest river in West Africa is the River Niger with a span of 418okm. River Niger is in Nigeria.

172) The Niger Delta is the second largest delta in the world. Niger Delta is in Nigeria.

173) Desert conditions occur in northern Africa, especially in the Sahara and the Sahel. Temperatures can range from 54° Celsius (130° F) on the hottest days to freezing on the coldest nights. Annual precipitation never exceeds 25 centimetres (10 inches), and some areas go without rain for years.

Culture

174) Men and women across East and Central Africa are often seen wearing brightly patterned cloths called Kanga.

175) Some of the most commonly spoken languages in Africa are Swahili, Amharic, Yoruba, Oromo, Hausa, Igbo, Zulu, Shona, Portuguese, French And English

176) Moroccans consider white to be the colour of mourning. A widow will wear all white for 40 days after her husband passes away.

177) African men can have multiple wives.

178) There are more than 3000 recognized ethnic tribes in Africa. Some of these are well-known, like the Zulu. While others keep to themselves and avoid contact with the modern world completely.

179) In Morocco, instead of the heart being considered a symbol of love, it's the liver. If someone states "You have conquered my liver" then, it's a match made in, well, Morocco.

180) Kidnapping your bride is a practise well known in the Sudanese Latuka tribe. When a young man wants to marry a girl, he kidnaps her from her home. It is after this act that he goes to visit the girl's father along with his

elder male relatives to ask for the blessing to marry. If dad agrees, he beats the suitor as a sign of his acceptance of the union. If he says 'no', the young man is at liberty to return the girl to her father's house or marry her as he so wishes.

181) Khweta Ceremony is a Southern African ceremony is practised by several tribes and is how a young boy proves his manhood. When they are of age, boys are sent to spend several days or weeks in a circumcision lodge during winter, where they're put through rigorous and often dangerous tests and rituals such as continuous dancing until exhaustion and circumcision.

182) Lobola is an ancient and controversial Southern African tradition in which the families of a bride and groom negotiate how much the groom must pay for the bride. All negotiations must be done in writing — never by phone or in person. The two families cannot even speak until negotiations are complete.

183) Members of the Maasai tribe in Kenya and Tanzania spit as a way of blessing. Men spit on new-borns and say they are bad in the belief that if they praise a baby, it will be cursed. Maasai warriors will also spit in their hands before shaking the hand of an elder.

184) To prove their manhood in the Ethiopian Hamer tribe, young boys must run, jump and land on the back of a bull

before then attempting to run across the backs of several bulls. They do this multiple times and usually in the nude.

185) The Ahaggaren Tuaregs of Algeria are part of a larger group of Berber-speaking Tuaregs. In their culture, the men wear veils almost all the time. However, they can take their veils off when inside family camps or while travelling.

186) In the Gio tribe in Ivory Coast, each wife has her own small house that she lives in with her children until they are old enough to move out. The children never live with their fathers.

187) In the South-western Congo, the Suku tribe honours ancestors and elders, when they die, with a ceremony held in the clearing of a forest. Here, gifts and offerings are brought, but outsiders and all women are forbidden to attend.

188) When male children reach age 5 or 6 in the Northern Angolan Songo tribe, they are sent to live with their uncles on their mother's side. This is because chiefs inherit their position through matrilineal lines.

189) In the Pokot tribe in Kenya, wealth is measured by how many cows a family has. Most Pokot people are either "corn people" or "cow people"— meaning that's what they cultivate on their land — but all Pokot people

measure their wealth by cows. The number of women a man can marry is determined by how many cows he has.

190) The Maasai people of Kenya and Tanzania have strict policies against killing wild animals. They keep cattle and livestock but leave wild animals untouched. In fact, each clan is associated with a specific wild species, which they often keep close to them and treat as a clan member.

191) The Himba people of Northern Namibia cover their skin with a mixture of butterfat and ochre — a natural earth pigment containing iron oxide — to protect themselves from the sun. For that reason, the Himba people often appear to have a red skin tone.

192) The San People of Botswana, also called Bushmen, are hunter-gatherers who were evicted from their ancestral land in the 1950s. They were forbidden to hunt and forced to apply for permits to enter reserves. The San switched to farming but they continued to gather herbs for medication and plants for food. Deprived of the ability to hunt, San numbers dwindled.

193) The Fulani tribe live in many countries in West Africa and follow a tradition called Sharo. Sharo happens when two young men want to marry the same woman. To compete for her hand, they beat one another up. The men

must suppress signs of pain and the one who takes the beating without showing signs of pain can take the wife.

194) The Chewa people are one of the largest indigenous groups of Malawi but live throughout Central and Southern Africa. When a person dies, one family tradition involves taking the body into the woods, slitting the throat, and forcing water through the body to cleanse it. They do this by squeezing the corpse's stomach until what comes out the rear end runs clear.

195) When a girl becomes a teenager in the Surma tribe of Southern Sudan, she begins the process of lip stretching. The girl has her bottom teeth removed to make space for a lip plate, which is increased in size annually.

196) The courtship dance of the Wodaabe - In a lot of African cultures woman gets to do pageantry, and the men get to choose their wives. It is the other way round in the Wodaabe tribe of Niger. The Wodaabe tribe of the Fulani has a cultural practice where the men play the display, and the women get to pick their husbands. The Guérewol is an annual ritual and competition that sees young men dress up in elaborate ornamentation and traditional face paint and gather in lines to dance and sing. In this particular tribe, the male beauty ideal is all about bright eyes and teeth, so men will often roll their eyes and bare their teeth to show off their sex appeal.

197) The lip plates of the Mursi - The Mursi tribe of Ethiopia is one of the last tribes in Africa where it's the norm for women to wear large pottery or wooden plates in their lower lips. When a Mursi girl reaches the age of 15 or 16, her lower lip is cut by her mother or another older woman in the settlement. The cut is held open by a wooden plug for about three months while it heals. Mursi members are rather egalitarian – girls are never forced to have their lip pierced; it's a personal choice.

198) The spitting of the Maasai - The Maasai people of Kenya and Northern Tanzania view spitting as a form of blessing and a sign of respect. The tribe's people use spitting to greet or say goodbye to friends clinch a bargain or to wish someone good luck. Two friends greeting each other will spit in their palms before shaking hands. When a baby is born, family members will spit on the child to wish him or her long life and good luck. Spitting is also customary on a daughter's wedding day, where her father will spit on her forehead to wish her a blessed union.

199) The healing dance of the San - This is one of the most magical traditions. For the San people of South Africa, Namibia, Botswana and Angola, dance is considered a sacred power. One of their most integral tribal traditions is the trance dance (also known as the healing dance).

The whole community comes together around a fire for several hours or even an entire night, led by healers and elders. The healers dance around the fire, chant and hyperventilate until they induce a powerful trance-like state. In this state, they are granted access to the spirit world (and are often able to walk over fire).

200) The wedding ceremony of the Ndebele - The Ndebele wedding ceremony is all about the bride – and her attire puts western white dresses to shame. This, in most part, is thanks to her future mother-in-law and the prettiest of all the tribal traditions. The groom's mother creates a Jocolo for the bride – an apron made of goatskin and decorated with gorgeous, colourful beads. The Jocolo is worn by all married women at the wedding ceremony and is representative of a mother surrounded by children. On their wedding day, the groom performs a ceremony in honour of his new wife, giving her thanks and credit for everything she's done for him in their time together.

201) Mourning a Death is tougher than fighting a lion - The Pokot tribe of Kenya has a radical view of death. They say it's easy to convince the Pokot into fighting a wild animal rather than to convince him into mourning or looking at a dead person. Whenever a person in a family is about to die, they abandon the house fearing if they even touch the person, they would be next to die.

202) There are thousands of indigenous languages and dialects spoken in Africa. Every African country has its own languages, even the smaller countries.

203) Africans are one of the biggest contributors to sculptural art. The art form of African sculpture dates back thousands of years with some of the earliest sculptures being found in Egypt.

204) Many people living in Eastern, Western and Southern African villages are farmers. They live almost entirely off the food they grow themselves. Traditional African food is also sold at outdoor markets.

205) Zulu ethnic group in South Africa is one of the most popular tribes in Africa. One reason why the tribe is so widely known is because of Shakaland, which is acknowledged worldwide as the birthplace of the legendary Shaka Zulu. With an estimated population of 11 million people, Zulu is known to be the largest ethnic group in South Africa.

Wildlife

206) Four of the five fastest land animals can be found in East Africa. These are the lion, the gazelle, the wildebeest, and the cheetah.

207) Africa is home to the largest land animal in the world – the African elephant.

208) It's also home to the tallest animal in the world – the giraffe.

209) As well as the fastest animal in the world – the cheetah.

210) The Big Five (lion, rhinoceros, elephant, leopard, and Cape buffalo) can be found in many places in Africa.

211) One of the largest nature reserves in the world is found in South Africa – The Kruger National Park.

212) The world's largest frog lives in Cameroon. It's named the Goliath Frog and it can grow to be more than 13 inches long.

213) Africa is home to 25% of the world's bird species. There are over 2500 kinds of birds found throughout its countries.

214) In Rwanda, you can go gorilla tracking. Tourists are taken into the mountains and shown gorillas in their

natural habitat. This raises money for the protection of these animals.

215) The Eco-region that straddles the Cameroon-Nigeria border is especially rich in forest butterfly species due to the favourable microclimate there.

216) Almost 100 species of lemurs are found in Madagascar.

217) The cold currents on South Africa's west coast make it the ideal home to the African Penguin.

218) Zambia has termite hills that get as large as houses.

219) Africa's deadliest animal is the hippopotamus. This is because it has caused the most human deaths.

220) Africa is home to the world's largest living land animal, the African elephant, which can weigh up to 7 tons.

221) The biggest five animal's - rhinos, leopards, lions, buffalo, and elephants can all be found in Kenya.

222) Each year, in the dry season (around July), a gigantic herd made up of millions of wildebeest migrates from Tanzania to Kenya, crossing the treacherous Mara River along the way. The Great Wildebeest Migration is a magnificent sight, and many come on safari just to see it.

223) Mount Kilimanjaro is Africa's highest peak, but it's also the tallest free-standing mountain in the world. The

dormant volcano is not part of a mountain range and stands on its own.

224) The Cousin Island in Seychelles is home to eleven endemic land-birds including the Seychelles Magpie-robin (Endangered), Seychelles Sunbird, Seychelles Fody and the Seychelles Blue-pige

225) Some landscapes are estimated to lose over 50 metric tonnes of soil per hectare per year due to neglect and desertification.

226) Over 30% of Africa's pastoral land and almost 20% of all forests and woodlands are classified as moderately- or heavily-degraded.

227) Deforestation rates in Africa are twice the average for the rest of the world with more than four million hectares of primary forest disappearing every year. Countries like Kenya, Malawi and Zambia have 1-5% of the primary forests remaining. Forests used to cover over 20% of Africa's 30 million square kilometres with almost all currently being destroyed and degraded by commercial and subsistence logging, as well as land conversion to plantations, agriculture, mines, roads and settlements.

228) Some 60% of the tropical forests in the Congo Basin are considered commercially exploitable.

229) Six of the top ten countries with the largest annual net loss of forested area are in Africa.

230) Primary forests shrink by on average 40,000 square kilometres (or 0.6% of total remaining forest cover) each year with most significant losses in heavily-forested countries such as the Democratic Republic of Congo and Gabon.

231) Over 1,270 large dams have been built along the continent's many rivers.

232) Lake Victoria is the largest lake in Africa and the second-largest freshwater lake in the world.

233) Africa has the most extensive biomass burning in the world, yet only emits about 4% of the world's total carbon dioxide emissions.

234) Africa has eight of the 11 major biomes and the largest-remaining populations of lion, elephant, rhinoceros, cheetah, hyena, leopard and hundreds of other species.

235) Megafauna like giraffe, zebra, gorilla, hippopotamus, chimpanzee and wildebeest are unique to the continent and only found here.

236) Lake Malawi has more fish species than any other freshwater system on earth.

237) Africa has over 85% of the world's elephants and over 99% of the remaining lions are on the African continent.

238) Eight of Conservation International's 34 biodiversity hotspots are in Africa.

239) The Serengeti (Tanzania) hosts the world's largest wildlife migration on Earth with over 750,000 zebra marching ahead of 1.2 million wildebeest as they cross this amazing landscape.

240) There are over 3,000 protected areas in Africa, including 198 Marine Protected Areas, 50 Biosphere Reserves, 129 UNESCO World Heritage Sites, and 80 RAMSAR "Wetlands of International Importance".

241) Africa has over 25% of the world's bird species.

242) Africa's extensive inland fisheries contain more than 3,000 fish species and account for two-thirds of global inland fish production.

243) Marine fisheries, the catch from Africa's inland fisheries are not exported. It is consumed almost entirely on the continent, forming a major source of people's protein intake.

Slavery

244) Slavery has existed in practically all civilizations. This was also the case in Africa before Arabs came and later the Europeans. In central East Africa, ethnic groups such as the Yao, Makua and Marava were fighting against each other and entire peoples within the continent traded with people they had captured through wars. It is important to emphasise the fact that the existing slavery in African before the Europeans came was not barbaric as European conducted it. In most cases, the cultures of slaves are similar to their captures and they did not use to be treated inhumanly and they were not regarded as property and sold as the Europeans did. As well, slaves were not subjected to the kind of hard labour like in the plantations in the Americas. The European slavery was notorious for its brutality and for the overcrowded, unsanitary conditions on slave ships, in which hundreds of Africans were packed tightly into tiers below decks for a voyage of about 5,000 miles (8,000 km).

245) The sale of African slaves became popular in between 15th and 17th century when Islam was gaining strength in North Africa. This was seven centuries before Europeans

explored the continent and ten centuries before West Africans were sold across the Atlantic to America.

246) The Atlantic slave trade started a lot earlier than you think. The Portuguese began trafficking African captives in the 1440s.

247) It wasn't initially a transatlantic trade. In the early days, enslaved Africans were brought to Portugal or to Atlantic islands like Madeira to work in agriculture.

248) Arab Muslims in North and East Africa sold captured Africans to the Middle East. There, they worked as field workers, teachers or harem guards, which is why the castration of male slaves was common practice.

249) Transatlantic Slave Trade (1440-1888) lasted for about 400years.

250) About 12.5 million slaves were captured from Africa and taken overseas in the 7th – 20th century.

251)As late as 1820, nearly four Africans had crossed the Atlantic for every European.

252) About four out of every five females that traversed the Atlantic were from Africa.

253) About 12.5 million slaves are estimated to have been embarked on ships. Many died, with only 10.7 million arriving in the Americas, and one in four slaving vessels failed to return to their homeport, victims of sea risks, rebellion and capture. No less than 26% on board were

classified as children (under 13 years and less than four feet four inches).

254) Over the 350-year history of the trans-Atlantic slave trade, captains purchased more adults (80%) than children (20%). Men were also prime, while African societies tended to retain females.

255) The average duration of the journey was just over two months, though a few voyages sailing from Upper Guinea could make a passage to the Americas in three weeks.

256) During the 16th to 19th centuries, Europeans were enslaved by Barbary pirates and sold to Northern Africans. This was known as the Barbary Slave Trade.

257) Between the 7th and 15th centuries, the external Muslim trading demand for African goods also included a demand for captives.

258) Forms of slavery have existed on all continents at different times in history – for instance, as a means of exploiting those captured in war – especially where there were labour shortages and an abundance of land. Slavery was certainly present in some African societies before the rise of Islam and Transatlantic slave trade.

259) Trans-Atlantic slavery was the largest long-distance coerced movement of people in history. After the collapse of the Amerindian population, the large number of enslaved Africans were transported to The Americas

(North, Central and South America). The enslaved Africans were mostly put to work in the plantations and mines of the European-run colonies.

260) One of the reasons for transporting enslaved Africans to the Americas was the tropical and semi-tropical nature of the area. The Europeans took advantage of several products that were hither unknown to Europeans, such as tobacco and sugar, which occupied a luxury niche in pre-expansion European tastes. There were problems of labour for producing these products in abundance. Africans was the target and the weakest to exploit.

261) There was some resistance. About 10% of slaving voyages experienced major rebellions, increasing the costs of a voyage. Some areas were noticeably more rebellion prone than others – Upper Guinea (Senegambia, Sierra Leone) – and have fewer slaves shipped away until it became economically justifiable to attempt it anyway.

262) Gorée Island in Senegal is a major tourist hotspot including for African-Americans. The Island was one of the main points of embarkation for slaves. Gorée has hosted a lot of high profile visitors such as US President Barack Obama and Nelson Mandela.

263) The top three embarkation points, which are, in order: Luanda in southern Africa, with 1.3 million slaves dispatched, Bonny in the Bight of Biafra, and Whydah on

the Slave Coast. The three ports together accounted for some 2.2 million slave departures.

264) The door of No Return is the final exit point of the slaves leaving Africa. One example is the House of Slaves (Maison des Esclaves). It is a museum and memorial to the Atlantic slave trade on Gorée Island, 3 km off the coast of the city of Dakar, Senegal. Its museum, which was opened in 1962 and curated until Boubacar Joseph Ndiaye's death in 2009. It is a memorialised enslaved Africa’s final point of exit.

265) David Eltis wrote about what it was like on a slave ship. Eltis writes. The sexes were separated, kept naked, packed close together, and the men were chained for long periods.

266) Throughout the slave trade era, filthy conditions ensured endemic gastrointestinal diseases, and a range of epidemic pathogens that, together with periodic breakouts of violent resistance, meant that between 12 and 13% of those embarked did not survive the voyage. The crew faced roughly the same poor survival odds, not to mention the risks of insurrections, successful ones of which were rare.

267) The slave trade affected the ethnic and racial identity of Africans.

268) The majority of African captives were transported not to the United States but Brazil followed by the Caribbean. A significant number of enslaved Africans arrived in the American colonies by way of the Caribbean, where they were "seasoned" and mentored into slave life. They spent months or years recovering from the harsh realities of the Middle Passage. Once they were forcibly accustomed to slave labour, many were then brought to plantations on American soil.

269) Slavery in America lasted for around 246 years. The institution of chattel slavery – the treatment of slaves as property – in the United States.1619 can be used as the beginning and the 1865 13th Amendment as its end. This period is 246 years.

270) By the 1480s, Portuguese ships were already transporting Africans for use as slaves on the sugar plantations in the Cape Verde and Madeira islands in the eastern Atlantic.

271) Spanish conquistadors took African slaves to the Caribbean after 1502, but Portuguese merchants continued to dominate the transatlantic slave trade for another century and a half, operating from their bases in the Congo-Angola area along the west coast of Africa.

272) The Dutch became the foremost slave traders during parts of the 1600s, and in the following century English

and French merchants controlled about half of the transatlantic slave trade, taking a large percentage of their human cargo from the region of West Africa between the Sénégal and Niger rivers.

273) Following capture, enslaved Africans were marched to the coast, a journey that could be as many as 300 miles (485 km). Typically, two captives were chained together at the ankle, and columns of captives were tied together by ropes around their necks.

274) An estimated 10 to 15 percent of the captives died on their way to the coast.

275) Historians estimate that between 15 and 25 percent of the African slaves bound for the Americas died aboard slave ships.

276) Occasionally, the African captives successfully revolted and took over the ships. The most famous such incident occurred when in 1839 a slave named Joseph Cinqué led a mutiny of 53 illegally purchased slaves on the Spanish slave ship Amistad, killing the captain and two members of the crew. The U.S. Supreme Court eventually ordered the Africans to be returned to their homes.

277) An incident occurred in slave ship Zong in 1781. Both Africans and crew members were dying of infectious disease, Capt. Luke Collingwood, hoping to stop the

disease, ordered that more than 130 Africans be thrown overboard. He then filed an insurance claim on the value of the murdered slaves.

278) One of the first martyrs to the cause of American patriotism was Crispus Attucks, a formerly enslaved man who was killed by British soldiers during the Boston Massacre of 1770. Some 5,000 Black soldiers and sailors fought on the American side during the Revolutionary War.

279) The 13th Amendment, adopted on December 18, 1865, officially abolished slavery in the USA.

280) Britain abolition of the slave trade came in1833, 32 years ahead of the US.

281) After Great Britain outlawed slavery throughout its empire in 1833, the British navy diligently opposed the slave trade in the Atlantic and used its ships to try to prevent slave-trading operations.

282) Brazil outlawed the slave trade in 1850, but the smuggling of new slaves into Brazil did not end entirely until the country finally enacted emancipation in 1888.

283) The Atlantic slave trade lasted longer than you imagine. The British abolished their slave trade in 1807; so did the Americans. The trade continued to flourish, however, down to the 1850s. The last known slave ship, which carried captives to Cuba, sailed in 1866.

Colonisation And Independence

284) Around 1854–74, France and Britain took the political initiatives of creating formal European colonies in Senegal, Lagos, and the Gold Coast.

285) For most of the 19th century the pressure to render the traditional African political order ineffective was predominantly from the British, but in the 1870s French companies began to offer effective competition to the British traders not only in Upper Guinea, where they had always been strong, but also on the Ivory Coast, in the ports immediately to the west of Lagos, and even in the lower river and delta of the Niger.

286) The French traders concentrated on the Sénégal River. France subsequently developed the colonies of Dahomey, the Ivory Coast, and French Guinea. From 1886 they also established formal authority over all other parts of the coastline that were not already claimed by the governments of Portugal or Britain.

287) In the 1870s, the British traders devoted their attention primarily to the active economies of the Niger delta, the Lagos hinterland, and the Gold Coast.

288) British interests were first maintained by an amalgamation of trading companies formed in 1879 by

Sir George Goldie to combat French commercial competition.

289) By the 1870s formal French and British armies had already ventured into the interior and had inflicted defeats on such major African powers as those of al-Ḥājj ʿUmar and Asante.

290) In 1879 Faidherbe's heirs on the Sénégal River had launched the thrust that was to take French arms conquering eastward across Sudan to Lake Chad and beyond.

291) What led to the Berlin West Africa Conference of 1884–85 has commonly been taken to be either the French reaction to the British occupation of Egypt in 1882 or the Congo basin rivalry between agents of France and Leopold II of the Belgians.

292) The German Empire established the protectorate of Togoland (in what is now the nation of Togo and most of what is now the Volta Region of Ghana) in 1884 during the period generally known as the "Scramble for Africa". It was British Togoland from 1916 to 1956 and French Togoland between 1916 and 1960.

293) Portuguese Guinea (Portuguese: Guiné), called the Overseas Province of Guinea from 1951, was a West African colony of Portugal from the late 15th century

until 10 September 1974, when it gained independence as Guinea-Bissau.

294) France claimed by far the larger amount of territory, nearly 1.8 million square miles compared with some 450,000 square miles in the four enclaves secured by Britain.

295) British territories contributed more economically than French Territories. The French Territories included a large part of the Sahara, and Sudan (modern Mali), Upper Volta (modern Burkina Faso), and Niger were by and large scantily populated and, remote from the coast.

296) The political boundaries established by the Europeans by 1898 (though usually not surveyed or demarcated on the ground until much later) largely determine the political map of western Africa today.

297) The only subsequent change of significance followed the British and French conquests of the German colonies during World War I (1914–18).

298) During the 1930s in Sierra Leone, European companies began to exploit extensive diamond-bearing gravels and to mine high-grade iron ore.

299) The first railway was built inland from Sekondi in the southeastern Gold Coast between 1898 and 1903 with the dual purpose of supporting gold mining and ensuring political control of Asante.

300) The end of the colonial period and the establishment during 1957–76 of all the former colonies as independent states was attributable both to a change in European attitudes toward Africa and the possession of colonies and to an African reaction to colonial rule born of the economic and social changes it had produced.

301) A 2014 YouGov poll revealed 59 per cent of British people view the British Empire as "something to be proud of." Those proud of their colonial history outnumber critics of the Empire three to one. Similarly, 49 per cent believe the Empire benefited its former colonies.

302) In the 1950s both American and European interests began to exploit Liberia's large-scale deposits of high-grade iron ore.

303) In 1948 universities were established in the Gold Coast and Nigeria; by 1960 the Gold Coast territory had about 4,500 university graduates and Nigeria more than 5,000.

304) The first French African university was a federal institution at Dakar opened in 1950; by 1960 the total number of graduates in French West Africa was about 1,800.

305) In 1946 politicians in French West Africa organized a federation-wide political association, the African Democratic Rally (RDA).

306) In 1947 the established politicians in Gold Coast brought in Kwame Nkrumah, who had studied in the United States and Britain and had been active in the Pan-African movement, to organize a nationalist party with mass support.

307) Nkrumah organized mass political party, able to win any general election, and during the following years, he negotiated with the British a series of concessions that resulted in 1957 in the Gold Coast becoming the independent state of Ghana.

308) African countries and the year they gain independence

COUNTRY	INDEPENDENCE DAY	COLONIAL NAME	COLONIAL RULERS
Algeria	July 5th, 1962		France
Angola	November 11th; 1975		Portugal
Benin	August 1st; 1960		French
Botswana	September 30th, 1966		Britain
Burkina Faso	August 5; 1960		France

COUNTRY	INDEPENDENCE DAY	COLONIAL NAME	COLONIAL RULERS
Cameroon	January 1st; 1960		French-administered UN trusteeship
Cape Verde	July 5th; 1975		Portugal
C. A. R	August 13th; 1960		France
Chad	August 11th, 1960		France
Comoros	July 6th; 1975		France
Congo	August 15th; 1960		France
Congo DR	June 30th; 1960		Belgium
Cote d'Ivoire	August 7th; 1960		France
Djibouti	June 27th; 1977		France
Egypt	February 28th, 1922		Britain
Eq Guinea	October 12; 1968		Spain
Eritrea	May 24th; 1993		Ethiopia
Ethiopia	over 2000 years, Never colonized	(formerly) Kingdom of Aksum	--
Gabon	August 17th; 1960		France

COUNTRY	INDEPENDENCE DAY	COLONIAL NAME	COLONIAL RULERS
Gambia	February 18th; 1965		Britain
Ghana	6 March 1957	Gold Coast	Britain
Guinea	October 2nd; 1958		France
Guinea Bissau	10 September 1974 24 September 1973		Portugal
Kenya	December 12th, 1963		Britain
Lesotho	October 4th; 1966		Britain
Liberia	July 26th; 1847		American colonization Society
Libya	December 24; 1951		Italy
Madagascar	June 26th; 1960		France
Malawi	July 6th; 1964		Britain
Mali	September 22nd; 1960		France
Mauritania	November 28th; 1960		France

COUNTRY	INDEPENDENCE DAY	COLONIAL NAME	COLONIAL RULERS
Mauritius	March 12th, 1968		Britain
Morocco	March 2nd; 1956		France
Mozambique	June 25th; 1975		Portugal
Namibia	March 21st; 1990		South African mandate
Niger	August 3rd; 1960		France
Nigeria	October 1st, 1960		Britain
Rwanda	July 1st; 1962		Belgium administered UN trusteeship
SaoTomePrincipe	July 12th; 1975		Portugal
Senegal	April 4th; 1960		France
Seychelles	June 29th; 1976		Britain
Sierra Leone	April 27th; 1961		Britain
Somalia	July 1st; 1960	British Somaliland Italian Somaliland	Britain Italy
South Africa	11 December 1931, April 1994(end of apartheid)	Union of South Africa	Britain

COUNTRY	INDEPENDENCE DAY	COLONIAL NAME	COLONIAL RULERS
Sudan	January 1st; 1956		Egypt, Britain
Swaziland	September 6th; 1968		Britain
Tanzania	April 26th, 1964		Britain
Togo	April 27th; 1960		French-administered UN trusteeship
Tunisia	March 20th; 1956		France
Uganda	October 9th; 1962		Britain
Zambia	October 24th; 1964		Britain
Zimbabwe	April 18th; 1980		Britain

Facts About Some of The Greatest Africans

309) Both Nelson Mandela and Desmond Tutu were influential South Africans who were awarded the Nobel Prize. They also happened to live on the same street at one time.

310) The author of the well-loved Lord of The Rings books, J.R.R Tolkien was a South African-born author from Bloemfontein, Free State.

311) Despotic Ugandan dictator, Idi Amin, had a slightly longer official title. It was: "His Excellency, President for Life, Field Marshal Al Hadji Doctor Idi Amin Dada, VC, DSO, MC, Lord of All the Beasts of the Earth and Fishes of the Seas and Conqueror of the British Empire in Africa in General and Uganda in Particular".

312) With a net worth of $16.1bn, Nigeria's Aliko Dangote is the richest Black person in the world.

313) Elon Reeve Musk is a business magnate, industrial designer and engineer. He founded and co-founded many companies including SpaceX and Tesla. He was born in Pretoria, South Africa.

314) Pasi William Sachiti is a Zimbabwean born British serial entrepreneur and inventor. He is founder and CEO of the driverless car manufacturer, Kar-go, which is known for being the UK start-up competing with multinational incumbents such as Google and Tesla, Inc.

315) Wangarĩ Muta Maathai was a renowned Kenyan social, environmental and political activist and the first African woman to win the Nobel Prize.

316) Nelson Mandela is an African legend. The symbol of Africa. Freedom fighter. He was a South African anti-apartheid revolutionary, political leader and philanthropist who served as President of South Africa from 1994 to 1999. He was the country's first black head of state and the first elected in a fully representative democratic election.

317) Kwame Nkrumah was a Former President of Ghana. He envisaged the African Union long before it became a reality. His footprints are still blueprints for us to follow.

318) Julius Nyerere was a Former President of Tanzania. A great leader who refused to allow the trappings of power to corrupt him. He was respected by his country, Africa and the rest of the world.

319) Félix Houphouët-Boigny was a politician and physician who was president of Côte d'Ivoire (Ivory Coast) from independence in 1960 until he died in 1993. Under his

rule, it became one of the most prosperous nations in sub-Saharan Africa.

320) Lumumba was a revolutionary Congo politician who helped the country to gain independence. He was the first Prime Minister of the Republic of Congo (now called D.R. Congo) from July to September of 1960. He acquired Belgian citizenship and worked as the president of a Congolese trade union. When he came back to Congo, Patrice Lumumba founded the Congolese National Movement (MNC).

321) Léopold Senghor, in full Léopold Sédar Senghor, was a poet, teacher, and statesman, first president of Senegal, and a major proponent of the concept of Negritude.

322) Sékou Touré, in full Ahmed Sékou Touré, was the first president of the Republic of Guinea (1958–84) and a leading African politician.

323) Martin Luther King was an African-American religious and political leader who changed the course of life for all African-Americans. His speech in 1968 "I have a dream" has become a classic.

324) Malcolm X was an African-American political leader. His resistance against racism helped African-Americans to realise their dream.

325) Shirley Ann Jackson, FREng is an American physicist and the eighteenth president of Rensselaer Polytechnic

Institute. She is the first African-American woman to have earned a doctorate at the Massachusetts Institute of Technology (MIT). She is also the second African-American woman in the United States to earn a doctorate in physics.

326) Kofi Annan's name cannot be skipped in any important list of African leaders. Even though he wasn't a mainstream politician, he was a world leader from Africa. Kofi Annan was a Ghanaian diplomat who led the United Nations (UN) as its 7th Secretary-General from 1997 to 2006.

327) Thomas Sankara is widely regarded as one of Africa's political heroes. He was a revolutionary who became Burkina Faso's president from 1983-1987. Sankara was a strong Pan-Africanist and a supporter of Marxism.

328) Muhammad Ali was an American professional boxer, activist and philanthropist. Nicknamed "the Greatest", he is widely regarded as one of the most significant and celebrated figures of the 20th century and as one of the greatest boxers of all time.

329) Bantu Stephen Biko was a South African anti-apartheid activist. Ideologically an African nationalist and African socialist, he was at the forefront of a grassroots anti-apartheid campaign known as the Black Consciousness Movement during the late 1960s and

1970s. His ideas were articulated in a series of articles published under the pseudonym Frank Talk.

330) Jomo Kenyatta - His name is one of the biggest in the history of African politics. Jomo Kenyatta was an anti-colonial activist who rose to become the first president of Kenya. He was also the first Prime minister of Kenya (1963-1964).

331) Sir Abubakar Tafawa Balewa, KBE PC (December 1912 – 15 January 1966) was a Nigerian politician who was the first Prime Minister of Nigeria.

332) Chief Obafemi Jeremiah Oyeniyi Awolowo, GCFR was a Nigerian nationalist and statesman who played a key role in Nigeria's independence movement, the First and Second Republics and the Civil War. The son of a Yoruba farmer, he was one of the truly self-made men among his contemporaries in Nigeria.

333) Muammar Muhammad Abu Minyar al-Gaddafi, commonly known as Colonel Gaddafi, was a Libyan revolutionary, politician and political theorist. He governed Libya as Revolutionary Chairman of the Libyan Arab Republic from 1969 to 1977 and then as the "Brotherly Leader" of the Great Socialist People's Libyan Arab Jamahiriya from 1977 to 2011.

334) Robert Gabriel Mugabe was a Zimbabwean revolutionary and politician who served as Prime

Minister of Zimbabwe from 1980 to 1987 and then as President from 1987 to 2017.

335) Ellen Johnson-Sirleaf - Africa's first female head of state's name cannot be omitted from this list. We still have some space to honour her and also to balance the political equation. Johnson-Sirleaf, commonly known as "Africa's Iron Lady", is a former Liberian president who was in office from 2006 to 2018. She is a Harvard graduate with an economics degree who fought hard from prisons and exile and became an inspiration to many young female politicians.

336) Kenneth Kaunda is a Zambian retired politician who became the country's first president from 1964-1991. As a teacher by profession, Kaunda gained a lot of political experiences when he served as a foreign affairs interpreter and adviser in 1949.

337) Haile Selassie, also known as Ras Tafari Makonnen, was an Ethiopian ruler (1916 to 1974) and emperor (1930-1974). Undoubtedly, Selassie was one of the biggest sons of Africa whose name can never be erased from history. Even at a young age, Selassie showed promising intellectual capacity.

338) Winnie Mandela was the most popular woman in Africa. South Africa political leader and former wife of Nelson Mandela.

339) Pele was an African-Brazilian footballer - the greatest. His feet and feats on the football pitch brought huge pride and honour to all blacks.

340) Bob Marley was a Jamaican musician and creative genius. He touched the hearts and minds of millions worldwide.

341)Olusegun Obasanjo was a President of Nigeria. A former military officer who voluntarily gave up power to civilians in 1979. He was returned to power in 1999 to save a worsening situation.

342) Sir Seretse Khama was Botswana's first president. He inherited an impoverished and little known obscure state and left an increasingly democratic and prosperous country.

343) Wole Soyinka is a Nigerian intellectual and writer. The first African Nobel laureate in literature, excelling as a playwright, poet and novelist – a vocal critic of Nigerian politics.

344) Dedan Kimathi was a Kenyan political leader who led the fight for independence from Britain. His ability to organise his people in the face of British colonialists was exemplary. He died a hero.

345) Fela Anikulapo-Kuti was a Great Nigerian Musician whose words have come to pass in African contemporary politics.

346) Jomo Kenyatta was Kenya's first president. He was a beacon and rallying point for the country's fight for independence. The father of modern Kenya.

347) Ken Saro Wiwa was a Nigerian writer and environmentalist who was executed for his beliefs. He aroused world attention to the plight of the oil-rich but poor Ogoni people.

348) Phillip Emeagwali was a Nigerian scientist domiciled in the USA. A supercomputer genius, he played a major role in making the internet a reality. His work has hugely benefited the oil industry.

349) Ahmed Baba - His full name Abu al-Abbas Ahmad al-Takruri Al-Massufi al-Tinbukti. He was a leader in the Songhai Empire that ruled approximately two-thirds of West Africa. Nowadays the areas are called Niger, Northern Nigeria, Gambia, Senegal, Guinea, Mauritania and Mali. The Empire collapsed due to the invasion of Europeans and Arab in 1591. All leaders including him were arrested and were taken to Sahara. He later died in 1627. He was also a renowned medieval West African Writer, Scholar, and political provocateur.

350) Almamy Suluku - He was a very powerful ruler who maintained hist independence for as long as possible. His kingdom was known as Biriwa. He became the war captain and made Biriwa one of the largest in Sierra

Leone. Biriwa became rich as he fostered trade in foodstuff, hides, ivory and gold. His name has gone down in history as one of the most powerful African leaders.

351) Behanzin Hossu Bowelle (The King Shark) - He was the most powerful king among the west African Kings during the last years of the 19th century. He was the master of the kingdom he ruled. If he nodded his head, he meant either death or life to his subjects. He overpowered the French expedition in 1890 and made them pay for using the Cotonou port. He was later defeated in 1894 by Colonel As. A. Dodds who was a Senegalese – European. He had been sent to fight against him and had been provided with every powerful French Armes forces. He died in 1906 when he was in Algeria.

352) Cetshwayo Kampande (Zulu King) - Cetshwayo kaMpande was the king of the Zulu Kingdom from 1873 to 1879 and its leader during the Anglo-Zulu War of 1879. His name has been transliterated as Cetawayo, Cetewayo, Cetywajo and Ketchwayo. He famously led the Zulu nation to victory against the British in the Battle of Isandlwana. He was a hero in a war against the British and he caused the biggest defeat which the English men had never had from any of the African leaders that opposed them. When the British invaded Zululand he defeated them and killed their heir to the French throne

by the name Prince Napoleon. He was later captured and imprisoned. He died in February in 1844.

353) Duse Mohamed Ali - Dusé Mohamed Ali was a Sudanese-Egyptian actor and political activist, who became known for his African nationalism. He was also a playwright, historian, journalist, editor, and publisher. He was among the Pan-Africanists as well as a supporter of Islam. He was the founder of the African Times and Orient Reviews in 1911. Its main objective was to spread the need for African Nationalism. He was an actor and wrote books in favour of Africans.

354) King Ibrahim Njoya - King Ibrahim Mbouombouo Njoya c. 1860 – c. 1933 in Yaoundé, was 17th in a long dynasty of kings that ruled over Bamum and its people in western Cameroon. Njoya's rule started during the 14th century. He was to become the king of the people of West Cameroon but he was not old enough to lead the people. Even after he matured he could not commence since his father's head was with enemies. According to the tradition of Bamum ancestors, skills or heads were of ceremonial importance and so he had to recover his father's head to commence. He died at an age of 73.

355) Omar Saidou Tall, born in Futa Tooro, Senegambia, was a West African political leader, Islamic scholar, Tijani Sufi and Toucouleur military commander who

founded a brief empire encompassing much of what is now Guinea, Senegal, and Mali.

The Spirituality Of Africa

by Jacob K. Olupona

356) African traditional religion refers to the indigenous or autochthonous religions of the African people. It deals with their cosmology, ritual practices, symbols, arts, society, and so on. Because religion is a way of life, it relates to culture and society as they affect the worldview of the African people.

357) Traditional African religions are not stagnant but highly dynamic and constantly reacting to various shifting influences such as old age, modernity, and technological advances.

358) Traditional African religions are less of faith traditions and more of lived traditions. They are less concerned with doctrines and much more so with rituals, ceremonies, and lived practices.

359) When addressing religion in Africa, scholars often speak of a "triple heritage," that is the triple legacy of indigenous religion, Islam, and Christianity that are often found side by side in many African societies.

360) While those who identify as practitioners of traditional African religions are often in the minority, many who

identify as Muslims or Christians are involved in traditional religions to one degree or another.

361)Though many Africans have converted to Islam and Christianity, these religions still inform the social, economic, and political life in African societies.

362) Traditional African religions have gone global! The Trans-Atlantic slave trade led to the growth of African-inspired traditions in the Americas such as Candomblé in Brazil, Santería in Cuba, or Vodun in Haïti. Furthermore, many in places like the US and the UK have converted to various traditional African religions, and the importance of the diaspora for these religions is growing rapidly. African religions have also become a major attraction for those in the diaspora who travel to Africa on pilgrimages because of the global reach of these traditions.

363) There are quite a number of revival groups and movements whose main aim is to ensure that the tenants and practice of African indigenous religion that is threatened survives. These can be found all over the Americas and Europe.

364) The concerns for health, wealth, and procreation are very central to the core of African religions. That is why they have developed institutions for healing, for commerce, and the general well-being of their practitioners and adherents of other religions as well.

365) Indigenous African religions are not based on conversions like Islam and Christianity. They tend to propagate peaceful coexistence, and they promote good relations with members of other religious traditions that surround them.

366) Today as a minority tradition, it has suffered immensely from human rights abuses. This is based on misconceptions that these religions are antithetical to modernity. Indeed indigenous African religions have provided the blueprint for robust conversations and thinking about community relations, interfaith dialogue, civil society, and civil religion.

367) Women play a key role in the practice of these traditions, and the internal gender relations and dynamics are very profound. There are many female goddesses along with their male counterparts. There are female priestesses, diviners, and other figures, and many feminist scholars have drawn from these traditions to advocate for women's rights and the place of the feminine in African societies. The traditional approach of indigenous African religions to gender is one of complementarity in which a confluence of male and female forces must operate in harmony.

368) Indigenous African religions contain a great deal of wisdom and insight on how human beings can best live

within and interact with the environment. Given our current impending ecological crisis, indigenous African religions have a great deal to offer both African countries and the world at large.

369) African indigenous religions provide strong linkages between the life of humans and the world of the ancestors. Humans are thus able to maintain constant and symbiotic relations with their ancestors who are understood to be intimately concerned and involved in their descendants' everyday affairs.

370) Unlike other world religions that have written scriptures, oral sources form the core of indigenous African religions. These oral sources are intricately interwoven into arts, political and social structure, and material culture. The oral nature of these traditions allows for a great deal of adaptability and variation within and between indigenous African religions. At the same time, forms of orature – such as the Ifa tradition amongst the Yoruba can form important sources for understanding the tenants and worldview of these religions that can serve as analogues to scriptures such as the Bible or the Qur'an.

Heritage Sites in Africa

Angola

371) **Mbanza Kongo, Vestiges of the Capital of the former Kingdom of Kongo** - Located in Zaire Province, Angola. The town of Mbanza Kongo, located on a plateau at an altitude of 570 metres, was the political and spiritual capital of the Kingdom of Kongo, one of the largest constituted states in Southern Africa from the 14th to 19th centuries.

Benin

372) **Royal Palaces of Abomey** - Located in Zou Department, Benin. The city held the seat of twelve kings who ruled the Kingdom of Dahomey between 1625 and 1900. All but one king built their palace within the area.

373) **W-Arly-Pendjari Complex** - This transnational extension (Benin, Burkina Faso) to the W National Park of Niger, inscribed in 1996 on the World Heritage List, cover a major expanse of intact Sudano-Sahelian savannah, with vegetation types including grasslands, shrublands, wooded savannah and extensive gallery forests. It includes the largest and most important

continuum of terrestrial, semi-aquatic and aquatic ecosystems in the West African savannah belt.

Botswana

374) **Okavango Delta -** Located in Botswana. This delta in north-west Botswana comprises permanent marshlands and seasonally flooded plains. It is one of the very few major interior delta systems that do not flow into a sea or ocean, with an almost intact wetland system. One of the unique characteristics of the site is that the annual flooding from the River Okavango occurs during the dry season, with the result that the native plants and animals have synchronized their biological cycles with these seasonal rains and floods. It is an exceptional example of the interaction between climatic, hydrological and biological processes. The Okavango Delta is home to some of the world's most endangered species of large mammals, such as the cheetah, white rhinoceros, black rhinoceros, African wild dog and lion.

375) **Tsodilo -** Located in North-West, Botswana. The site features more than 4,500 rock art paintings in the Kalahari Desert. Archaeological records provide evidence of human and environmental activities ranging over 100,000 years.

Burkina Faso

376) **Ancient Ferrous Metallurgy Sites of Burkina Faso -** This property is composed of five elements located in different provinces of the country. It includes about fifteen standing, natural-draught furnaces, several other furnace structures, mines and traces of dwellings. Douroula, which dates back to the 8th century BCE, is the oldest evidence of the development of iron production found in Burkina Faso.

377) **Ruins of Loropéni -** Located in Loropéni, Burkina Faso. More than a thousand years old, Loropéni is the best-preserved of ten fortresses in Lobi, which were part of about a hundred stone enclosures built during the trans-Saharan gold trade.

378) **W-Arly-Pendjari Complex** - This transnational extension (Benin, Burkina Faso) to the W National Park of Niger, inscribed in 1996 on the World Heritage List, cover a major expanse of intact Sudano-Sahelian savannah, with vegetation types including grasslands, shrublands, wooded savannah and extensive gallery forests. It includes the largest and most important continuum of terrestrial, semi-aquatic and aquatic ecosystems in the West African savannah belt.

Cabo Verde

379) **Cidade Velha, Historic Centre of Ribeira Grande -** Located in Ribeira Grande, Cape Verde. The town, in the south of the island of Santiago, was the first European colonial outpost in the tropics, with remains dating back to the 16th century. Two churches, a royal fortress, and Pillary Square help comprise the tropical town's original street layout.

Cameroon

380) **Dja Faunal Reserve** - Located in Dja-et-Lobo and Haut-Nyong, Cameroon. Among Africa's largest and best-protected rain forests, the Cameroonian reserve is almost completely surrounded by the Dja River and contains 107 mammal species, of which five are threatened.

381) **Sangha Trinational** - Situated in the north-western Congo Basin, where Cameroon, Central African Republic and Congo meet, the site encompasses three contiguous national parks totalling around 750,000 ha. Much of the site is unaffected by human activity and features a wide range of humid tropical forest ecosystems with rich flora and fauna, including Nile crocodiles and goliath tigerfish, a large predator. Forest clearings support herbaceous

species and Sangha is home to considerable populations of forest elephants, critically endangered western lowland gorilla, and endangered chimpanzee. The site's environment has preserved the continuation of ecological and evolutionary processes on a huge scale and great biodiversity, including many endangered animal species.

The Central African Republic

382) **Manovo-Gounda St. Floris National Park** - Located in Bamingui-Bangoran, Central African Republic. The park features vast savannahs with a wealth of flora and fauna, such as black rhinoceros, elephants, cheetahs, leopards, wild dogs, red-fronted gazelles and buffalo. The site was placed on the List of World Heritage in Danger in 1997 due to grazing and poaching that is thought to have claimed 80% of the wildlife in the park. Also cited was the shooting of four park staff and "a general state of deteriorating security".

383) **Sangha Trinational** - Situated in the north-western Congo Basin, where Cameroon, Central African Republic and Congo meet, the site encompasses three contiguous national parks totalling around 750,000 ha. Much of the site is unaffected by human activity and features a wide range of humid tropical forest ecosystems with rich flora

and fauna, including Nile crocodiles and goliath tigerfish, a large predator. Forest clearings support herbaceous species and Sangha is home to considerable populations of forest elephants, critically endangered western lowland gorilla, and endangered chimpanzee. The site's environment has preserved the continuation of ecological and evolutionary processes on a huge scale and great biodiversity, including many endangered animal species.

Chad

384) **Ennedi Massif** - Natural and Cultural Landscape - Located in Chad. In the northeast of the country, the sandstone Ennedi Massif has been sculpted over time by water and wind erosion into a plateau featuring canyons and valleys that present a spectacular landscape marked by cliffs, natural arches and pitons.

385) **Lakes of Ounianga** - Located in Ennedi Region, Chad. The Lakes of Ounianga are a series of 18 lakes located in the Sahara desert, in North-Eastern Chad. They exhibit a variety of sizes, depths, chemical compositions and colourations, and some of them are home to aquatic fauna.

Congo

386) **Sangha Trinational** - Situated in the north-western Congo Basin, where Cameroon, Central African Republic and Congo meet, and the site encompasses three contiguous national parks totalling around 750,000 ha. Much of the site is unaffected by human activity and features a wide range of humid tropical forest ecosystems with rich flora and fauna, including Nile crocodiles and goliath tigerfish, a large predator. Forest clearings support herbaceous species and Sangha is home to considerable populations of forest elephants, critically endangered western lowland gorilla, and endangered chimpanzee. The site's environment has preserved the continuation of ecological and evolutionary processes on a huge scale and great biodiversity, including many endangered animal species.

Côte d'Ivoire

387) **Comoé National ParkIn** - Located in Zanzan, Côte d'Ivoire. Among the largest protected sites of West Africa, the park features the Comoé River and the unique flora which accompanies it. The site was placed on UNESCO's List of World Heritage in Danger in 2003, due to unrest in Côte d'Ivoire, and various other factors

such as poaching, wildfires, lack of proper management of the site, and overgrazing.

388) **Historic Town of Grand-Bassam** - Located in Sud-Comoé, Côte d'Ivoire. A colonial town built during the 19th and 20th centuries, Grand-Bassam was the first Ivorian capital following French rule in the region. Its quarters, which specialised in commerce, administration and general housing, helped the city become the economic and judicial hub of the country, in addition to being its most important port.

389) **Mount Nimba Strict Nature Reserve** - Located on the borders of Guinea, Liberia and Côte d'Ivoire, Mount Nimba rises above the surrounding savannah. Its slopes are covered by dense forest at the foot of grassy mountain pastures. They harbour an especially rich flora and fauna, with endemic species such as the viviparous toad and chimpanzees that use stones as tools.

390) **Taï National Park** - Located in Guiglo and Sassandra, Côte d'Ivoire. One of the few remaining sections of the West African tropical forest, the park features a rich flora, including eleven species of monkeys.

The Democratic Republic of the Congo

391) **Garamba National Park** - Located in Orientale, Democratic Republic of the Congo. The park has vast savannahs, grasslands and woodland, featuring elephants, giraffes, hippopotamuses and the white rhinoceros. Garamba was deemed to be endangered following the diminution of the white rhinoceros population in the area, but it was removed from the list in 1991. However, it later regained the status in 1996, when three rangers were killed and the population of white rhinoceros fell once again.

392) **Kahuzi-Biega National Park** - Located in Maniema and South Kivu, the Democratic Republic of the Congo. The park is dominated by two extinct volcanoes, Kahuzi and Biega. It also has abundant fauna, including the graueria gorillas. The park was deemed to be endangered in 1997 when deforestation and hunting became a major problem. Militia groups and illegal settlers were also settling in the park, while fire and poaching helped justify the World Heritage Committee's decision.

393) **Okapi Wildlife Reserve** - Located in Orientale, Democratic Republic of the Congo. Covering a fifth of the Ituri Rainforest in the Congo River basin, the reserve contains many threatened species of primates and birds. It

is inhabited by the nomadic pygmy Mbuti and Efé tribes. In 1997, looting, the killing of elephants, and the departure of reserve staff led the World Heritage Committee to place the reserve on its List of World Heritage in Danger, only a year following its inscription as a natural heritage site.

394) **Salonga National Park -** Located in Maniema and South Kivu, the Democratic Republic of the Congo. Africa's largest tropical rain forest reserve is situated at the heart of the Congo River basin and only accessible by water. It is the habitat of endangered species such as the bonobo, the Congo peafowl, the forest elephant, and the slender-snouted crocodile. The site was deemed to be in danger in 1999, due to increased poaching activities and encroachments.

395) **Virunga National Park -** Located in North Kivu and Orientale, the Democratic Republic of the Congo. The park comprises swamps, savannahs, and snowfields.

Eritrea

396) **Asmara -** A Modernist African City - Located in Maekel, Eritrea. Located at over 2000 metres above sea level, the capital of Eritrea developed from the 1890s onwards as a military outpost for the Italian colonial

power. After 1935, Asmara underwent a large scale programme of construction applying the Italian rationalist idiom of the time to governmental edifices, residential and commercial buildings, churches, mosques, synagogues, cinemas, hotels, etc.

Ethiopia

397) **Aksum** - Located in Tigray Region, Ethiopia. The ruins of the city of Aksum, dating from the 1st to the 13th century, mark the heart of ancient Ethiopia and what was the "most powerful state between the Eastern Roman Empire and Persia". It includes monolithic obelisks, giant stelae, royal tombs, and ruins of former castles.

398) **Fasil Ghebbi, Gondar Region** - Located in Amhara Region, Ethiopia. The fortress was the residence of the Ethiopian emperors during the 16th and 17th century. The city remains, which feature buildings with Hindu and Arab influences, were later remodelled with Baroque-style architecture by Jesuit missionaries.

399) **Harar Jugol, the Fortified Historic Town** - Located in Harari Region, Ethiopia. The city is on a plateau and surrounded by gorges and savannah. It contains 82 mosques, 102 shrines, and unique interior design in the

townhouses. It is said to be the fourth-holiest city of Islam.

400) **Konso Cultural Landscape** - Located in Southern Nations, Nationalities, and People's Region, Ethiopia. The site features 55 kilometres (34 mi) of stonewalled terraces and fortified settlements in the Konso highlands of Ethiopia.

401) **Lower Valley of the Awash** - Located in Afar Region, Ethiopia. Paleontological findings from at least four million years ago, such as Lucy, give evidence of human evolution.

402) **Lower Valley of the Omo** - A prehistoric site near Lake Turkana, the lower valley of the Omo is renowned the world over. The discovery of many fossils there, especially Homo gracilis, has been of fundamental importance in the study of human evolution.

403) **Rock-Hewn Churches, Lalibela** - Located in Amhara Region, Ethiopia. The site contains eleven medieval cave churches from the 13th century. Simien National Park.

404) **Tiya** - Located in Southern Nations, Nationalities, and People's Region, Ethiopia. The archaeological site contains 36 monuments, which includes 32 carved stelae covered with symbols hard to decrypt.

Gabon

405) **Ecosystem and Relict Cultural Landscape of Lopé-Okanda** - Located in Ogooué-Ivindo and Ogooué-Lolo, Gabon. The park features well-preserved tropical rain forests and savannah, resulting in a diverse ecosystem consisting of endangered, large mammals.

Gambia

406) **Kunta Kinteh Island** - Located in Banjul, Lower Niumi, and Upper Niumi, Gambia. The site is a testimony to the encounters between Africa and Europe from pre-colonial times to independence along the Gambia River.

407) **Stone Circles of Senegambia** - The site consists of four large groups of stone circles that represent an extraordinary concentration of over 1,000 monuments in a band 100 km wide along some 350 km of the River Gambia. The four groups, Sine Ngayène, Wanar, Wassu and Kerbatch, cover 93 stone circles and numerous tumuli, burial mounds, some of which have been excavated to reveal material that suggests dates between 3rd century BC and 16th century AD. Together the stone circles of laterite pillars and their associated burial mounds present a vast sacred landscape created over

more than 1,500 years. It reflects a prosperous, highly organized and lasting society.

Ghana

408) **Asante Traditional Buildings -** Located in Kumasi, Ghana - The site, north-east of Kumasi, hosts the final intact remains of the Ashanti Empire, which peaked in the 18th century. The dwellings, which are made of earth, wood, and straw, are susceptible to the damages caused by the "onslaught of time and weather."

409) **Forts and Castles, Volta, Greater Accra, Central and Western Regions -** The site features the remains of fortified trading posts, built along the Ghanaian coast between 1482 and 1786.

Guinea

410) **Mount Nimba Strict Nature Reserve -** Located on the borders of Guinea, Liberia and Côte d'Ivoire, Mount Nimba rises above the surrounding savannah. Its slopes are covered by dense forest at the foot of grassy mountain pastures. They harbour an especially rich flora and fauna, with endemic species such as the viviparous toad and chimpanzees that use stones as tools.

Kenya

411) **Fort Jesus, Mombasa** - Located in Mombasa, Kenya. Fort Jesus is a Portuguese fort built from 1593 to 1596 on Mombasa Island to guard the old port of Mombasa, Kenya. The site's layout follows the Renaissance ideal that the human body is perfectly proportionate.

412) **Kenya Lake System in the Great Rift Valley** - Located in Rift Valley Province, Kenya. Located in the Great Rift Valley, Kenya, the site features three lakes: Lake Bogoria, Lake Nakuru and Lake Elementaita. A highly diverse population of birds, including thirteen threatened species, frequent the area.

413) **Lake Turkana National Parks** - Located in Lake Turkana, Kenya. Turkana, as Africa's largest saline lake, is an important area for the study of fauna and flora. It is a breeding ground for the Nile crocodile, hippopotamus and several venomous snakes. The site was placed on the List of World Heritage in Danger in 2018, primarily due to the potential impact of Ethiopia's Gilgel Gibe III Dam.

414) **Lamu Old Town** - Located in Lamu, Kenya. The town is the oldest Swahili settlement and is built in coral stone and mangrove timber. It features inner courtyards, verandas, and elaborate wooden doors.

415) **Mount Kenya National Park/Natural Forest** - At 5,199 m, Mount Kenya is the second-highest peak in Africa. It is an ancient extinct volcano, which during its period of activity (3.1-2.6 million years ago) is thought to have risen to 6,500 m. There are 12 remnant glaciers on the mountain, all receding rapidly, and four secondary peaks that sit at the head of the U-shaped glacial valleys. With its rugged glacier-clad summits and forested middle slopes, Mount Kenya is one of the most impressive landscapes in East Africa.

416) **Sacred Mijikenda Kaya Forests** - Located in Coast Province, Kenya. The site comprises eleven forests spread 200 km (120 mi) along the coast of Kenya. They hold the remains of villages built during the 16th century by the Mijikenda and are now considered sacred sites.

417) **Thimlich Ohinga Archaeological Site** - Located in Migori County, Kenya. Dating back to the 16th century CE, the dry-stone walled settlement is the largest and best-preserved traditional enclosures of its kind.

Lesotho

418) **Maloti-Drakensberg Park** - The Maloti-Drakensberg Park is a transnational property composed of the uKhahlamba Drakensberg National Park in South Africa

and the Sehlathebe National Park in Lesotho. The site has exceptional natural beauty in its soaring basaltic buttresses, incisive dramatic cutbacks, and golden sandstone ramparts as well as visually spectacular sculptured arches, caves, cliffs, pillars and rock pools. The site's diversity of habitats protects a high level of endemic and globally important plants. The site harbours endangered species such as the Cape vulture (Gyps coprotheres) and the bearded vulture (Gypaetus barbatus).

Madagascar

419) **Rainforests of the Atsinanana** - Located in Eastern Madagascar, Madagascar. The site consists of six national parks and protects the island's unique biodiversity, which has evolved in isolation for 60 million years. The park was deemed to be in danger in 2010, when logging and hunting activities continued to escalate, despite a ban by Madagascar on exporting illegal timber.

420) **Royal Hill of Ambohimanga** - Located in Antananarivo, Madagascar. The royal city and burial site is a spiritual and sacred site which has created strong feelings of national identity for several centuries.

421)**Tsingy de Bemaraha Strict Nature Reserve** - Located in Melaky, Madagascar. The canyon of the Manambolo River comprises karstic and limestone landscapes cut into peaks and a forest of limestone needles. It also holds undisturbed forests, lakes and mangrove swamps, which are the habitat for lemurs and birds.

Malawi

422) **Chongoni Rock-Art Area** - Located in Dedza District, Malawi. The 127-site area contains the richest concentration of rock art in Central Africa, ranging from Stone Age paintings to contemporary work from farmers. The symbols depicted in rock art are strongly centred on women and retain a cultural significance for the Chewa.

423) **Lake Malawi National Park** - Located in Central Region and Southern Region, Malawi. Lake Malawi contains hundreds of fish species, mostly endemic.

Mali

424) **Cliff of Bandiagara (Land of the Dogons)** - Located in Bandiagara Cercle, Mali. The sandy plateau and cliffs of Bandiagara outline the site, featuring houses, granaries, altars, sanctuaries, and Togu-Na meeting-places. Age-old social traditions such as masks, feasts,

rituals, and ancestral worship also add to its cultural significance.

425) **Old Towns of DjennéI** - Located in Djenné, Mali. Inhabited since 250 BCE, the city was an important link in the trans-Saharan gold trade. It contains 2,000 traditional houses.

426) **Timbuktu** - Located in Timbuktu Cercle, Mali. The city was a centre for the propagation of Islam in the 15th and 16th centuries and features three mosques and many madrasahs. The sites were deemed endangered after the Battle of Gao in June 2012, which followed several weeks of constant threats to the area. Days later, some sites within Timbuktu were destroyed by Ansar Dine, an Islamist group, citing religious reasons.

427) **Tomb of Askia** - Located in Gao Region, Mali. Built-in 1495, the pyramid was built as a tomb for Emperor Askia Mohamed. It represents the power of an empire that controlled the trans-Saharan gold trade. The site was deemed endangered after the Battle of Gao in June 2012, which followed several weeks of constant threats to the area.

Mauritius

428) **Aapravasi Ghat -** Located in Port Louis District, Mauritius. Aapravasi Ghat was the first site chosen by the British government to take part in the "Great Experiment", where indentured labourers were used instead of slaves. Between 1834 and 1920, almost half a million contracted workers passed through Port Louis from India, either to work in Mauritius or to transfer to other British colonies.

429) **Le Morne Cultural Landscape -** Located in Rivière Noire District, Mauritius. The rugged mountain that juts into the ocean was used as a shelter by runaway slaves through the 18th and early 19th centuries. They formed small settlements in the caves and on its summit.

Mozambique

430) **Island of Mozambique -** Located in Nampula, Mozambique. The fortified former Portuguese trading post has used the same architectural techniques, style, and materials since the 16th century.

Namibia

431) **Namib Sand Sea** - Located in Namibia. Namib Sand Sea is the only coastal desert in the world that includes extensive dune fields influenced by fog. Covering an area of over three million hectares and a buffer zone of 899,500 hectares, the site is composed of two dune systems, an ancient semi-consolidated one overlain by a younger active one.

432) **Twyfelfontein or |Ui-||ais** - Located in Kunene, Namibia. The site has one of the largest concentrations of rock engravings in Africa, which range from a period of over 2,000 years.

Niger

433) **Air and Ténéré Natural Reserves** - Located in Arlit Department, Niger. Africa's largest protected area, located in the Saharan desert of Ténéré, consists of the volcanic rock mass of Air and a small isolated Sahelian pocket with unique flora and fauna. The natural reserve was placed on UNESCO's List of World Heritage in Danger in 1992, due to the increase in military conflicts and the hostage-taking of six reserve staff in February. Removal from this list was considered in 1999, but as of 2011, its position remains unchanged.

434) **Historic Centre of Agadez -** Located in Tchirozerine Department, Niger. Known as the gateway to the desert, Agadez, on the southern edge of the Sahara desert, developed in the 15th and 16th centuries when the Sultanate of Aïr was established and Touareg tribes were sedentarized in the city, respecting the boundaries of old encampments, which gave rise to a street pattern still in place today.

435) **W-Arly-Pendjari Complex -** Located in Benin; Burkina Faso; Niger. The parks are in the zone between savanna and forest lands and are an important ecosystem for the biogeographical area.

Nigeria

436) **Osun-Osogbo Sacred Grove -** Located in Oshogbo, Nigeria. The dense forest of the Osun Sacred Grove, on the outskirts of the city of Oshogbo, is one of the last remnants of primary high forest in southern Nigeria. Regarded as the abode of the goddess of fertility Osun, one of the pantheons of Yoruba gods, the landscape of the grove and its meandering river is dotted with sanctuaries and shrines, sculptures and artworks in honour of Osun and other deities. The sacred grove, which is now seen as a symbol of identity for all Yoruba

people, is probably the last in Yoruba culture. It testifies to the once widespread practise of establishing sacred groves outside all settlements.

437) **Sukur Cultural Landscape** - Located in Madagali, Nigeria. The site features the Palace of the Hidi, terraced fields, and the remains of the former iron industry.

Senegal

438) **Bassari Country:** Bassari, Fula and Bedik Cultural Landscapes. Located in Senegal. The site, located in south-east Senegal, includes three geographical areas: the Bassari–Salémata area, the Bedik–Bandafassi area and the Fula–Dindéfello area, each with its specific morphological traits. The Bassari, Fula and Bedik peoples settled from the 11th to the 19th centuries and developed specific cultures and habitats symbiotic with their surrounding natural environment.

439) **Djoudj National Bird Sanctuary** - Located in Saint-Louis Region, Senegal. The Senegal River delta wetland area consists of streams, lakes, ponds and backwaters. It is the home to 1.5 million birds, including the great white pelican, the purple heron, the African spoonbill, the great egret, and cormorants. The sanctuary also features

crocodiles, African manatees, and other typical Sahelian species.

440) **Island of Gorée -** The island of Gorée lies off the coast of Senegal, opposite Dakar. From the 15th to the 19th century, it was the largest slave-trading centre on the African coast. Ruled in succession by the Portuguese, Dutch, English and French, its architecture is characterized by the contrast between the grim slave-quarters and the elegant houses of the slave traders. Today it continues to serve as a reminder of human exploitation and as a sanctuary for reconciliation.

441) **Island of Saint-Louis -** Located in Saint-Louis Region, Senegal. The French colonial settlement from the 17th century is on an island in the mouth of the Sénégal River. It played an important role in the culture and economy of West Africa.

442) **Niokolo-Koba National Park -** Located in a well-watered area along the banks of the Gambia River, the gallery forests and savannahs of Niokolo-Koba National Park have a very rich fauna, among them Derby elands (largest of the antelopes), chimpanzees, lions, leopards and a large population of elephants, as well as many birds, reptiles and amphibians.

443) **Saloum Delta -** Located in Senegal. Fishing and shellfish gathering have sustained human life in the 5,000

km properties, which is formed by the arms of three rivers. The site comprises brackish channels encompassing over 200 islands and islets, mangrove forest, an Atlantic marine environment, and dry forest. The site is marked by 218 shellfish mounds, some of them several hundred metres long, produced by its human inhabitants over the ages.

444) **Stone Circles of Senegambia** - The site consists of four large groups of stone circles that represent an extraordinary concentration of over 1,000 monuments in a band 100 km wide along some 350 km of the River Gambia. The four groups, Sine Ngayène, Wanar, Wassu and Kerbatch, cover 93 stone circles and numerous tumuli, burial mounds, some of which have been excavated to reveal material that suggests dates between 3rd century BC and 16th century AD. Together the stone circles of laterite pillars and their associated burial mounds present a vast sacred landscape created over more than 1,500 years. It reflects a prosperous, highly organized and lasting society.

Seychelles

445) **Aldabra Atoll** - Located in Aldabra Group, Seychelles. The Aldabra Atoll consists of four large coral

islands and a lagoon, surrounded by a coral reef. The islands are home to the world's largest population of giant tortoises.

446) **Vallée de Mai Nature Reserve** - Located in Praslin, Seychelles. In the heart of the small island of Praslin, the reserve has the vestiges of a natural palm forest preserved in almost its original state. The famous coco de mer, from a palm-tree once believed to grow in the depths of the sea, is the largest seed in the plant kingdom.

South Africa

447) **Barberton Makhonjwa Mountains** - Located in Mpumalanga, South Africa. The mountains contain the world's oldest geological structures and are known to have preserved volcanic and sedimentary rocks estimated to be between 3.6 and 3.25 billion years old.

448) **Cape Floral Region Protected Areas** - Located in Eastern Cape and Western Cape, South Africa. The site consists of eight protected areas that are among the richest in plant life worldwide, containing nearly 20% of Africa's total flora. Its scientific value is demonstrated by the presence of fire and radiation adaptivity in plants and seed dispersal by insects.

449) **ISimangaliso Wetland Park** - Located in KwaZulu-Natal, South Africa. The park features a variety of landforms, including coral reefs, long sandy beaches, coastal dunes, lake systems, and papyrus wetland, caused by fluvial, marine and Aeolian processes.

450) **Maloti-Drakensberg Park** - The Maloti-Drakensberg Park is a transnational property composed of the uKhahlamba Drakensberg National Park in South Africa and the Sehlathebe National Park in Lesotho. The site has exceptional natural beauty in its soaring basaltic buttresses, incisive dramatic cutbacks, and golden sandstone ramparts as well as visually spectacular sculptured arches, caves, cliffs, pillars and rock pools. The site's diversity of habitats protects a high level of endemic and globally important plants. The site harbours endangered species such as the Cape vulture (Gyps coprotheres) and the bearded vulture (Gypaetus barbatus)

451) **Mapungubwe Cultural Landscape** - Located in Limpopo, South Africa. The open savannah landscape lies at the confluence of the Limpopo and Shashe Rivers. It was the heart of the Mapungubwe Kingdom until the 14th century, when the area was abandoned, leaving untouched remains of palaces and settlements.

452) **Richtersveld Cultural and Botanical Landscape** - Located in Northern Cape, South Africa. The

mountainous desert sustains the semi-nomadic livelihood of the Nama, which includes seasonal migrations that have gone unchanged for two millennia.

453) **Robben Island** - Robben Island was used at various times between the 17th and 20th centuries as a prison, a hospital for socially unacceptable groups and a military base. Its buildings, particularly those of the late 20th century such as the maximum-security prison for political prisoners, witness the triumph of democracy and freedom over oppression and racism.

454) **Vredefort Dome** - Located in Free State and North West, South Africa. The crater, with a diameter of 190 km (120 mi), is the largest, oldest, and most deeply eroded astrobleme found on Earth, dating back more than two billion years.

455) **ǂKhomani Cultural Landscape** - Located in Northern Cape, South Africa. The ǂKhomani Cultural Landscape is located at the border with Botswana and Namibia in the northern part of the country, coinciding with the Kalahari Gemsbok National Park (KGNP). The large expanse of sand contains evidence of human occupation from the Stone Age to the present and is associated with the culture of the formerly nomadic ǂKhomani San people and the strategies that allowed them to adapt to harsh desert conditions.

Togo

456) **Koutammakou, the Land of the Batammariba** - Located in Kara Region, Togo. The Batammariba's mud tower houses have become a symbol of Togo. They range up to two stories and feature spherical granaries.

Uganda

457) **Bwindi Impenetrable National Park** - Located in south-western Uganda, at the junction of the plain and mountain forests, Bwindi Park covers 32,000 ha and is known for its exceptional biodiversity, with more than 160 species of trees and over 100 species of ferns. Many types of birds and butterflies can also be found there, as well as many endangered species, including the mountain gorilla.

458) **Rwenzori Mountains National Park** - Located in Bundibugyo District, Kabarole District, and Kasese District, Uganda. Covering most of the Rwenzori Mountains, including Mount Margherita, Africa's third-highest peak, the park features glaciers, waterfalls and lakes in an Alpine landscape. It also features various endangered species and unusual flora.

459) **Tombs of Buganda Kings at Kasubi** - Located in Kampala District, Uganda. The tombs, built after 1884,

are a major example of prime architecture using organic materials, principally wood, thatch, reed, and wattle and daub. The tombs were almost completely destroyed by a fire in March 2010, prompting the World Heritage Committee to reluctantly mark the site as being in danger. The Ugandan government has since called for the reconstruction of the tombs, and UNESCO has agreed to mobilise funds for the project.

United Republic of Tanzania

460) **Kilimanjaro National Park -** Located in Kilimanjaro Region, Tanzania. The volcanic massif Mount Kilimanjaro is Africa's highest point at 5,895 metres (19,341 ft.) and is surrounded by a park with savannah and forest featuring numerous mammals.

461) **Kondoa Irangi Rock Paintings -** Located in Kondoa district, Tanzania. Two millennia of rock carving, many of high artistic value, have been found at 150 shelters in the site. They tell the tale of socio-economic development from hunter-gatherer to agro-pastoralism.

462) **Ngorongoro Conservation Area -** Located in Arusha Region, Tanzania. The site features a concentration of wild animals in a crater beside the active volcano Oldonyo Lengai.

463) **Ruins of Kilwa Kisiwani and Ruins of Songo Mnara** - Located in Kilwa District, Tanzania. The site features the remains of two ports used extensively for trade across the Indian Ocean from the 13th and 16th century.

464) **Selous Game Reserve** - Large numbers of elephants, black rhinoceroses, cheetahs, giraffes, hippopotamuses and crocodiles live in this immense sanctuary, which measures 50,000 km2 and is relatively undisturbed by human impact. The park has a variety of vegetation zones, ranging from dense thickets to open wooded grasslands.

465) **Serengeti National Park** - The vast plains of the Serengeti comprise 1.5 million ha of savannah. The annual migration to permanent water holes of vast herds of herbivores (wildebeest, gazelles and zebras), followed by their predators, is one of the most impressive natural events in the world.

466) **Stone Town of Zanzibar** - The Stone Town of Zanzibar is a fine example of the Swahili coastal trading towns of East Africa. It retains its urban fabric and townscape virtually intact and contains many fine buildings that reflect its particular culture, which has brought together and homogenized disparate elements of

the cultures of Africa, the Arab region, India, and Europe over more than a millennium.

Zambia

467) **Mosi-oa-Tunya / Victoria Falls** - These are among the most spectacular waterfalls in the world. The Zambezi River, which is more than 2 km wide at this point, plunges noisily down a series of basalt gorges and raises an iridescent mist that can be seen more than 20 km away.

Zimbabwe

468) **Great Zimbabwe National Monument** - Located in Masvingo Province, Zimbabwe. The city, now in ruins, was an important trading centre between the 11th and 15th centuries and was capital of the Bantu civilization.

469) **Khami Ruins National Monument** - Khami, which developed after the capital of Great Zimbabwe had been abandoned in the mid-16th century, is of great archaeological interest. The discovery of objects from Europe and China shows that Khami was a major centre for trade over a long period of time.

470) **Mana Pools National Park, Sapi and Chewore Safari Areas** - Located in Mashonaland West,

Zimbabwe. The park, located on the banks of the Zambezi River, features a variety of wild animals, such as buffalo, leopards, cheetahs and Nile crocodiles.

471) **Matobo Hills** - Located in Matabeleland South, Zimbabwe. The large boulders have been used as natural shelters since the early Stone Age and feature a collection of rock paintings.

472) **Mosi-oa-Tunya / Victoria Falls** - Located in Livingstone District and Matabeleland North, Zambia, Zimbabwe. The falls of the Zambezi River, which is more than 2 km (1.2 mi) wide, plunge various basalt gorges resulting in a colourful mist.

African Best Artists

473) OGA STEVE ABAH, PLAYWRIGHT (Nigeria)

Oga Steve Abah is a tireless, prolific theatre activist whose work focuses on creating dramas based on the everyday lives of ordinary people: poor, powerless, without a channel for learning to cope with the pressures of contemporary life. In his work, he aims for a creative, aesthetic "empowering" theatre practice drawing on masquerade and dance, the existing forms of performance of both peasant society and urban workers. Through this technique, people address the inequalities in their lives and create exquisite dramas in open-air settings all over Africa.

474) CHINUA ACHEBE, AUTHOR (Nigeria)

The father of the African novel, Achebe made his literary debut in 1958 with the classic Things Fall Apart, which has been translated into 50 languages. It is hard to resist his beguiling style, which infuses Standard English with Igbo proverbs and speech patterns. As the founding editor of Heinemann's African writers' series, he was instrumental in introducing the world to new writings from Africa. Also an essayist, writer of short stories and university professor, he continues to inspire and teach, despite having been paralysed in a car accident in 1990. He could be considered literary godparent to several fledgeling novelists (including Chimamanda Ngozi Adichie, the writer of Purple Hibiscus). In 2004, he declined to accept Nigeria's second-highest honour in protest at the state of affairs in his country. Many believe a Nobel Prize would be a more appropriate honour.

475) DAVID ADJAYE, ARCHITECT (Tanzania)

The 40-year-old is the head of Adjaye/ Associates, having received his Masters in architecture in 1993 from the Royal College of Art. Based in London, Adjaye has received commissions all over Europe and the United States. His work strives to create a sense of dialogue between the building and its space. He has given lectures around the world and has worked for the BBC, notably hosting a six-part TV series, Dream spaces, about modern architecture. His company's designs include the east London projects Elektra House in Whitechapel and Idea Store in Poplar, and the Nobel Peace Centre in Oslo.

476) NEWTON ADUAKA, FILM DIRECTOR (Nigeria)

Born in Ogidi, eastern Nigeria, in 1966, Newton Aduaka moved to Lagos in 1970 and then to England in 1985. After a diploma in video arts and post-production, he studied at the London International Film School, graduating in 1990. He wrote and published short stories while working as a sound mixer on a wide range of productions. In 1997, he set up Granite Film Works with Maria Elena L'Abbate to produce cutting-edge, uncompromising films. His debut feature Rage (2000) was released to acclaim, becoming the first independent film by a black film-maker to gain a national release in Britain. It won many festival prizes, including best director at the Pan African Film * * Festival in Los Angeles and the Oumarou Ganda Award at Fespaco, Africa's biggest film festival. Aduaka has directed commercials and several short films. Funeral (2002) was commissioned for the Cannes Film Festival alongside similarly-themed work from directors such as Walter Salles, Arturo Ripstein and Amos Gitai. The short film Aicha (2004) demonstrates his poetic and visual skills in telling a story.

477) MAHMOUD AHMED, MUSICIAN (Ethiopia)

Little known outside his native country, Mahmoud Ahmed was born in the Mercato district of Addis Ababa and spent his formative years listening to music by the Imperial Body Guard Band and the famous Ethiopian singer Tlahoun Gessesse, before heading into the capital and shining shoes for a living. He found a job at the Arizona club, one of few "semi-legal" clubs permitted by Emperor Haile Selassie, which became a favourite haunt of the Imperial Body Guard Band, whom he eventually joined before recording in his own right. He was rediscovered by the West through the ground-breaking Ethiopiques series released by Buda Musique in the late 1990s.

478) AMA ATA AIDOO, PLAYWRIGHT (Ghana)

Ama Ata Aidoo is best known for her play Anowa, a complex tale of a husband and wife's relationship set against the background of the iniquities of the slavery and the disapproval of her conservative, resentful mother. Initially strong, Anowa eventually succumbs to madness and death as her husband finds himself disempowered by her strength. Aidoo's work, published in the 1960s, was ahead of its time, pointing to the contradictions and tensions in love and the abuse of power; her husband Kofi employs slave labour in their business, a practice Anowa despises.

479) AMADOU AND MARIAM, MUSICIANS (Mali)

Success was a long time coming for this talented, award-winning Malian couple who met in 1977 at the Institute for the Blind in Bamako. The guitarist and singer Amadou Bagayoko had served his apprenticeship by playing guitar in legendary band Les Ambassadeurs. After moving to Abidjan, Ivory Coast, in 1986, they recorded a series of cassette-only releases that made them stars in their homeland. These were recently re-released on the French label Because Records (1990-1995: The Best of the African Years). They recorded three successful major-label albums after moving to Paris in the late 1990s before meeting up with Manu Chao, who produced their biggest and (by general agreement) best album so far, Dimanche á Bamako.

480) AYI KWEI ARMAH, AUTHOR (Ghana)

Born in 1939, and one of only a few Ghanaian novelists who have been published internationally since the 1960s, Ayi Kwei Armah is rather less known but is no less talented than his more widely feted Nigerian contemporaries. Variously based over the years in the United States, Algeria, Paris, Tanzania and Senegal, Armah has gathered a dedicated fan-base who might wish that his output had been somewhat greater than it has been. However, he has also worked as a translator, editor, scriptwriter and teacher. His novel The Beautiful Ones Are Not Yet Born burst on to the scene in 1968, to be followed by others that display his extraordinary way with prose, at once excoriating and spiritual: Two Thousand Seasons (1973), Osiris Rising: A Novel of Africa Past, Present and Future (1995) and The Healers (2000).

481) LES BALLETS AFRICAINS, DANCERS AND MUSICIANS (Guinea)

The Guinean choreographer Keita Fodeba formed the dance company in Paris in 1952. They successfully toured the world until Guinea's independence in 1958. On returning to their native country, the company became a national treasure; Les Ballets Africains, affectionately known as "roving ambassadors", are credited with enlightening their audiences about Guinean culture. The company strives to foster a better understanding of Africa and build relationships with other countries. Their lively music is made by drums, flutes and Guinean castanets; audiences enjoy their elaborate costumes, dance and storytelling.

482) BIYI BANDELE, AUTHOR (Nigeria)

Born in 1967, Bandele is one of the most versatile and prolific of the UK-based Nigerian writers, having turned his hand to theatre, journalism, television, film and radio, as well as the fiction with which he first made his name. His novels, which include The Man Who Came In From the Back of Beyond (1991) and The Street (2000), are rewarding reading, capable of wild surrealism and wit, as well as political engagement, as is all his writing. As a playwright, his ambition is admirable.

483) SOKARI DOUGLAS CAMP, ARTIST (Nigeria)

Sokari Douglas Camp is one of the first female African artists to have attracted the attention of the European art market. She left her country at the age of 21 to study in Oakland, California and at the London Royal College of Art. Her expressive man-high steel sculptures show her immediate relationship to her home country. She uses masks and ritual clothing as compositional themes in her work, reflecting the political and cultural relationship between Africa and the Western world.

484) BOYZIE CEKWANA, CHOREOGRAPHER AND DANCER (South Africa)

The choreographer works mainly in South Africa but also presents a lot of work in Europe, mostly in France. Cekwana has taken contemporary dance to the next level in Africa. He is important because he has changed perceptions about dance, particularly in South Africa. Trained in classical ballet, he found his own way of blending the heritage of his country with his work. He deals with identity and history, fusing politics with the mainstream of art and finding his South African forms within the classical form.

485) SOULEYMANE CISSE, FILM DIRECTOR (Mali)

Cissé has crafted a body of films that combine visual elegance with Marxist ideology and allegorical storytelling. His best-known film is Yeelen ("Brightness"), a Jury Prize-winner at Cannes in 1987 and one of the great experiences of world cinema. Born in 1940, Cissé began his career as a projectionist and photographer in Mali. After studying cinema in the Soviet Union for seven years, he returned to Mali, where he made newsreels and documentaries. His first fiction film, Cinq jours d'une vie ("Five Days in a Life", 1972), launched his career and gained attention for the burgeoning African film movement. In 1975, Cissé directed the first feature film in his native language of Bambara, The Girl, only to have the film banned. Drawing on indigenous lifestyles and folklore, Cissé attempts to explore conflicts in Malian society.

486) LUEEN CONNING, PLAYWRIGHT (South Africa)

In her play A Coloured Place, Conning has produced an exciting piece of writing that explores the contradictions inherent in being "coloured" in post-apartheid South Africa. Using multi-media staging, the play is unrelenting as its barrage of images, perceptions and attitudes spill out on to the stage from bodiless voices.

487) TSITSI DANGAREMBGA, AUTHOR (Zimbabwe)

When Dangarembga's first book, Nervous Conditions, won the Commonwealth Writers Prize for Fiction in 1989, Doris Lessing wrote: "Many good novels written by men have come out of Africa, but few but black women. This is the novel we have been waiting for... it will become a classic." It was read by millions and was among the top 12 titles in the project to identify Africa's 100 best books of the 20th century. The follow-up has been long coming (Dangaremgba turned her attention to film), but The Book of Not, just published by Ayebia Clarke Publishing, was worth the wait; it's a powerful story spanning the period from minority rule to the emergence of independent Zimbabwe.

488) TOUMANI DIABATE, MUSICIAN (Mali)

Perhaps the best-known kora player in the world, the Malian star Toumani Diabaté has released a string of albums alongside the likes of Ballake Sissoko (New Ancient Strings) and the late, great Ali Farke Touré (In the Heart of the Moon). Refusing to be pigeonholed, he's worked with the blues legend Taj Mahal and Spanish superstars Ketama, and is always willing to mix various styles with his Malian roots. This year saw the release of the critically acclaimed Boulevard de 'Independance with his band Symmetric Orchestra. Recorded at the same time as In the Heart of the Moon, it showcases the diversity of his playing.

489) DILOMPRIZULIKE, ARTIST (Nigeria)

Dilomprizulike, the self-proclaimed "junkman of Africa", is among the most enigmatic of artists. Dilom creates sculpture and performances tied deeply into traditional African masquerade, yet which are informed by a post-modern awareness. Dilom is art. He lives in what seems to be a junkyard in a permanent performance, recycling the detritus of Lagos into artwork, clothes, a home and a way of life that questions much of what we take for granted. Yet the work wrought from rubbish is deeply beautiful, intriguing and has a real gravitas; he is a philosophical Gaudi for the 21st century.

490) CESARIA EVORA, SINGER (Cape Verde)

This Grammy-winning singer hails from the port town of Mindelo, on Sao Vincente. She possesses one of the most powerful and alluring voices in the world, helped by a bitter-sweet style of singing called morna, a descendent of Portuguese fado, sung in Creole-Portuguese. Ostensibly a folk singer (although the style is known as Cape Verdean blues), she's accompanied by guitar, accordion, violin, cavaquinho (a small four-string guitar) and clarinet, and often sings of isolation, love and slavery.

491) SAMUEL FOSSO, PHOTOGRAPHER (Cameroon)

Samuel Fosso is a prolific and witty photographer, whose colourful and outlandish portraits range from African chiefs to

American women. But they all have one thing in common; on close inspection, they can be seen to be self-portraits. His explorations of identity have featured in the Guggenheim in New York and the Photographers' Gallery in London

492) FLORA GOMES, FILM DIRECTOR (Guinea-Bissau)

Gomes is the only film-maker to emerge from Guinea-Bissau, a former Portuguese colony in West Africa. He attended a course in cinematography at the Institute of Cuban Art in Havana under the legendary Santiago Alvarez and qualified as a cameraman and director of photography in 1972. Gomes started working for television with the late Senegalese film-maker Paulin Vieyra. In 1973, he made his first news film about the second congress of PAIGC (African Party for the Independence of Portuguese Guinea and Cape Verde). In 1983, he made Mortu Nega, the first full-length film produced in Guinea-Bissau, a remarkable tale of love during the liberation and the struggles of independence.

493) PIERRE ATEPA GOUDIABY, ARCHITECT (Senegal)

Through the African Scholarship Program, Goudiaby took a degree in architecture from the Rensselaer Polytechnic Institute in New York in 1973. Born in the village of Baila, his humble beginnings are a thing of the past; he is now among Africa's most respected and successful architects. His company, Atepa

Group, is responsible for some of the most innovative and modern buildings in Senegal. His West Africa Central Bank in Dakar is modelled on the baobab tree. Elders in his culture gather around this sacred tree and have discussions. In 2003, the Africa-America Institute awarded Goudiaby the Special Recognition Award for Architecture and Business Enterprise in Africa.

494) MAHAMAT SALEH HAROUN, FILM DIRECTOR (Chad)

Born in N'Djamena in 1961, Haroun was forced to leave his home country at the start of the 1980s because of civil war, fleeing to Cameroon and later Paris. He studied in France - film, then journalism - and worked for five years as a reporter before directing his first short film in 1994. Among his early shorts are Maral Tanie (1994) and Goi-Goi, le nain (1995). His first documentary, Bord d'Africa (1995), focuses on African musicians living in Bordeaux. The second, Sotgui Kouyaté, un griot modern (1996), tells the story of a griot from Burkina Faso. The film explores the life of the famous griot in the different worlds of Africa and Europe. Haroun provides a new language and aesthetic for African cinema. Bye Bye Africa (1999) was the first film of its kind to be produced entirely in Chad; it's a "documentary fiction", a story about making a documentary in which he himself plays an exiled African film-maker. His latest film is Daratt ("Dry Season").

495) DELIA JARRETT-MACAULEY, AUTHOR (Sierra Leone)

Drawing on her Sierra Leonian background for an uplifting story about a child soldier, Moses, Citizen & Me (2005), Jarrett-Macauley's confident first novel did not enjoy the sort of hype that greeted, say, Helen Oyeyemi. But a measure of her accomplishment in dealing with sensitivity, humour and empathy with disturbing material is that the novel won the George Orwell Prize for political writing. Already the author of The Life of Una Marson, 1905-65, a biography of the first black programme-maker at the BBC, Jarrett-Macauley exemplifies the African diasporic talent that has continued to invigorate mainstream English literature.

496) SALIF KEITA, MUSICIAN (Mali)

One of the founders of Afro-pop, Keita was born in Mali in 1949 to a noble family. He was born an albino, which led his mother to hide him for fear of reprisals from superstitious neighbours. His decision to become a singer met with hostility from his family because it was seen as an occupation beneath his noble standing. He stuck to his guns and left his village for the capital Bamako aged 18. He later played with the Rail Band and Les Ambassadeurs before becoming a solo artist, recording such classics as Soro and the Grammy-nominated Amen.

497) KHALED, MUSICIAN (Algeria)

Possibly the most famous Algerian rai singer of all time, Khaled is one of the few North African artists to have won wide acclaim, particularly in his adopted home of France, where his singles "Aicha" and "Didi" flew to the top of the charts. Born Khaled Hadj Brahim in Sidi-El-Houri in 1960, he left school at 16 to record his first single. Influenced by Arabic, Spanish and French music, as well as The Beatles and James Brown, his sound soon typified rai's smooth synth-pop output of the Eighties. Moving to France in 1986, he recorded a string of successful albums such as Kenza and Sahra before going back to his roots with his latest, Ya-Rayi.

498) ABDOULAYE KONATE, ARTIST (Mali)

The contemporary artist, 53, began his career as a graphic designer at the Musée National in Bamako and went on to be appointed director of the Palais de la Culture. In 2002, he received two awards: the Chevalier d'Ordre National du Mali and Chevalier de l'Ordre des Arts et des Lettres de France. Having started as a painter, his style has evolved into multi-medium and large installation work. His political, social and environmental views are expressed through his art. Recently, his work has depicted the devastating effects of Aids on society and individuals.

499) KONONO NO 1, MUSICIANS (Congo)

Konono No 1 are a unique musical collective from Kinshasa. They use percussion instruments salvaged from junkyards, and combine electric likembé (a thumb piano) with percussion and voices, filtered through a PA system that consists of a microphone carved out of wood, fitted with a magnet from a car alternator and an oversized horn-shaped amp. The cacophony is unforgettable.

Likembé player Mawangu Mingiedi is the leader of the band. A former truck driver, now in his seventies, he adapts trance-inducing Zombo ritual music (from his homeland near the Angolan border), as heard on the band's critically acclaimed album Congotronics.

500) FEMI KUTI, MUSICIAN (Nigeria)

He'll never quite escape the shadow of his father (the Afro-beat legend Fela Kuti), but Femi Anikulapo Kuti has done a creditable job of emulating his father's work, albeit in a much cleaner (and less risqué) way. Kuti was born in London in 1962 but grew up in Nigeria's former capital, Lagos. He quickly adapted to his new musical and politically active surroundings, learning various instruments as well as singing. He put this education to good use on a series of albums with his band Positive Force. He headlines the African Soul Rebels Tour next year.

501) FAUSTIN LINYEKULA, CHOREOGRAPHER AND DANCER (Congo)

Born in Ubunvu in north-east Congo, Faustin Linyekula doesn't conform to any form or structure or place. He's inspired by nothing and creates something out of it. Coming from Congo, he's always worked under very difficult circumstances, but for him, these circumstances have become a form of inspiration. After eight years in self-imposed exile (1993-2001), Linyekula returned to his homeland with a renewed desire to create art there and established a company, Les Studios Kabako, in Kinshasa. His work can best be described as experimental performance art, using text and theatre to examine the links between art and society and issues of identity.

502) VINCENT MANTSOE, CHOREOGRAPHER AND DANCER (South Africa)

Vincent Mantsoe grew up dancing in the township of Soweto and trained at the Moving Into Dance School in Johannesburg. He is the pioneer of Afro-fusion - a blend of African aesthetics and traditions with European forms - bringing it to the world stage. His work draws on traditional African dance, the song and dance rituals of the sangomas (traditional healers) as well as modern, ballet and Asian forms.

503) ZOLA MASEKO, FILM DIRECTOR (South Africa)

During apartheid, the handful of South Africa's black film-makers were either unable to work in their country or were in exile. The end of apartheid provided opportunities to make films that were in synch with their history and realities. Maseko became the first South African to win the Etalon de Yennega, Africa's leading prize for a fiction film, at Fespaco (2005) with his biopic Drum on the life and death of the journalist Henry Nxumalo. Maseko was born in exile in 1967 and educated in Swaziland and Tanzania. He studied at the National Film School at Beaconsfield, England. He also directed an 11-part series for the South African Broadcasting Corporation entitled In Search of Our History. The capturing of popular memory lies at the heart of his work.

504) SOUAD MASSI, SINGER (Algeria)

This talented singer/songwriter fled her homeland after being hounded out by Islamic fundamentalists who took exception to her promotion of independence for young women. She ended up in Paris, where she started to create her own unique blend of folk, rock, flamenco and shaabi (Arabic street pop), releasing her acclaimed debut album Raoui ("Storyteller") in 2001. She's toured prolifically for the past few years and won a Planet Award at the 2006 BBC world music awards. She is defiantly outspoken about the problems in Algeria: "Remaining silent would mean that terrorists have won and that all the intellectuals they murdered died for nothing," she says.

505) YOUSSOU N'DOUR, MUSICIAN (Senegal)

Perhaps the best-known African singer of all, most people remember N'Dour for his hit "7 Seconds" with Neneh Cherry, but there is much more to him. With his band Super Etoile de Dakar, he changed the face of Senegalese music with a radical form of energetic, polyrhythmic music called mbalax, which spread across West Africa like wildfire. He's become a figurehead for Africa, campaigning for Aids awareness and speaking against corruption and genocide. His finest albums remain Immigrés and the Grammy-winning Egypt, a devotional album in praise of Islamic sages.

506) KETTLY NOEL, CHOREOGRAPHER AND DANCER (Haiti/Mali)

Kettly Noël, from Port au Prince, Haiti, began dancing seriously at the age of 17. In 1996, she moved to Benin, where she began giving training in contemporary dance to local youngsters, many of whom went on to become members of the Benin National Ballet. At the end of 1999, Noël relocated to Mali, intending to start a similar project there. She's a female choreographer who deals with women's issues in Africa. Her work deals with identity and the fight for the position of women in the continent. She confronts issues other people are not willing to go near in their work. She likes to go deeply into dark areas in search of light.

507) IDRISSA OUEDRAOGO, FILM-MAKER (Upper Volta/Burkina Faso)

Born in Banfora in 1954, Ouedraogo's early knowledge of film came from the travelling cinemas that visited villages. He made his mark at the Cannes Film Festival with his 1990 film Tilai, which won the Jury Prize. His 1989 film Yaaba about a 10-year-old boy who befriended an older woman remains an international success. Having studied film in Paris, his style is dubbed "Francophone African cinema". His films are known for their visual charm and the attention he pays to the composition of each scene.

508) TRACEY ROSE, ARTIST (South Africa)

Tracey Rose makes Tracey Emin look like a Girl Guide. Rose is a mixed-race feminist who uses identity and sexual politics as incendiary devices, waging war on her fellow South Africans' sensibilities with almost narrative-less performances, films and artworks. It is hard to resist the crazy world she weaves, a car crash of popular culture and extreme sociology, so assuredly absurd that it has a kind of convincing intoxication that pulls you in. Even against a backdrop of the extremes of her home town Johannesburg, she is wild, seeming to weave visual poetry across the polarities of South Africa's political landscape that can make you laugh, yet feel guilty for your collusion.

509) IBRAHIM EL SALAHI, ARTIST (Sudan)

It is difficult not to fall in love with the deeply serene El Salahi, the godfather of African modernism. He has created great work over five decades, has had as many chapters to his practice as Picasso, and has generated his own personal art-history. There's a story that when he worked as the Sudanese cultural minister in the Seventies he was imprisoned for six months, accused by the military dictator of anti-government activities. In prison, he asked the guard for paper and pencils. The guard laughed: "You're not in New York now!" Salahi managed to beg and steal the means to paint and draw, under threat of being beaten or worse. His work helps one to see why someone might be driven to take such risks.

510) OUSMANE SEMBENE, FILM-MAKER (Senegal)

Sembène is the "father" of African cinema. Best known for his historical-political works with strong social comment, Sembène was born in Senegal in 1923. He left school at 15 and worked as a plumber, bricklayer and apprentice mechanic. In 1944, he was called up to active duty to liberate France and was subsequently sent to the colony of Niger. After his discharge, he took part in the Dakar-Niger railroad strike, which inspired his book Les bouts de Bois de Dieu ("God's Bits of Wood") (1960). In 1948, Sembène went back to France, worked in Marseilles docks, became a trade union activist and joined the French Communist Party. In 1956, his first book Le docker noir ("The Black

Docker") was published. Sembène began to realise the greater potential of cinema for a largely illiterate mass audience. He went to Moscow to study under Mark Donskoj at the Gorky Studios). His short film Borom Sarret (1963) is the cornerstone on which African cinema has been built.

511) ABDERRAHMANE SISSAKO, FILM DIRECTOR (Mauritania/Mali)

Sissako is the most distinguished and inventive film-maker working in Africa today. Born in Kiffa, Mauritania, in 1961 and raised in Mali, his father's homeland, he returned to Mauritania in 1980. The difficulties of adjustment encouraged him to turn to literature and film. A study grant allowed him to attend the Institute of the University of Moscow. Le Jeu (1990), first presented as a graduation assignment, won the best short prize at the Giornate Del Cinema Africano of Perugia in 1991. In 1993, Octobre was shown at Locarno and won prizes the world over. Waiting for Happiness was screened at Cannes 2002 and won the best film in the Un Certain Regard section. It was shown at the New York Film Festival in 2002 and won the Grand Prize at Fespaco in 2003. His latest film Bamako, in which Western financial institutions are put on trial by African civil society, had its premiere in Cannes in May this year and its UK premiere at the London Film Festival last month.

512)WOLE SOYINKA, DRAMATIST, NOVELIST, POET (Nigeria)

Soyinka is an iconic figure who, in 1986, became the first black (and first African) Nobel laureate. Outspoken against government oppression in his native Nigeria (like his cousin Fela Kuti), his writing career over 40 years has encompassed prison, exile and a death sentence for treason. He is the best-known playwright from the continent. His plays include Death and the King's Horseman, an exploration of morality, human weakness and pomposity within the performance of sacrificial rituals. Some of his most important writing is as an autobiography, such as his 1970s prison memoir The Man Died and Aké: A Childhood Memoir. As a novelist, he is less accessible.

513)RACHID TAHA, MUSICIAN (Algeria)

Taha is the perfect foil to the sugary love songs sung by many modern rai artists. His music emulates the guttural, promiscuous and socially satirical rural rai style typified by the late great Cheikha Remitti, and also the shaabi singer Dahmane El Harrachi, whose song "Ya Rayah" he covered for his biggest hit. Taha started out in the French rock band Carte De Séjour, where his politically charged lyrics took shape. A string of solo albums followed, bursting with traditional Algerian rhythms and a healthy punk-rock attitude. His best-loved album Diwan, covering classic Algerian songs, was recently followed up with Diwan 2.

514) NGUGI WA THIONG'O, AUTHOR (Kenya)

Exiled from Kenya for 22 years because of his highly political work (including the best-selling novel Petals of Blood), one of Africa's greatest and most highly respected writers has just returned to attention with his first novel in 20 years, Wizard of the Crow, a magisterial, acerbic milestone work set in a fictional modern African state.

515)TINARIWEN, MUSICIANS (Mali)

Formed in 1982 in Muammar Gaddafi's Tuareg rebel camps, this celebrated Tuareg blues band gave up guns for guitars, singing in French and Tamashek and playing a style of music called tishmoumaren ("music of the unemployed"). Their creative heart is the vocalist and guitarist Ibrahim Ag Alhabib, who can strike a mean Chuck Berry riff. The band's first album, The Radio Tisdas Sessions, recorded in 2000, was followed by Amassakoul ("Traveller") in 2004. Their third album Aman Iman: Water Is Life is released in January on Independiente.

516) ROKIA TRAORE, MUSICIAN (Mali)

One of the most distinctive new voices of Mali, and a tremendous live performer, Rokia Traoré came to UK attention at Womad in 2000. Although not a griot, her family encouraged her to sing at weddings, though her father was a wealthy diplomat and such things were frowned upon. While studying in France she sang with a rap group, and this led her to begin writing songs. She was discovered on the French festival circuit, and in 1997 became a protégé of Ali Farka Touré, who persuaded her to record her first album Mouneissa. A series of critically acclaimed albums have followed.

517)BINYAVANGA WAINANA, AUTHOR (Kenya)

Born in Kenya, but with an imagination that transcends borders and cultures, Wainana won the Caine Prize for African Writing (the "African Booker") in 2002. His Granta-published essay, "How to Write about Africa", brilliantly satirising the clichés and stereotypes that can ensnare non-African writers, will make any but the guilty laugh out loud. As the founder of the journal Kwani, he nurtures new writers, including Yvonne Adhiambo Owuor, the 2004 Caine winner.

518) ZOLA, MUSICIAN (South Africa)

Born in Soweto, Bonginkosi Dlamini, known as Zola, is one of the most famous singers of kwaito (a form of dance music pitched somewhere between house and hip-hop). He performed the score and appeared in the Oscar-winning film Tsotsi. His father abandoned his mother and their three children in one of the roughest and most notorious areas, where unemployment, violence, alcoholism and drugs were rife. This helped him prepare for his role as the gangster Papa Action in Yizo Yizo 2. His music reflects his tough upbringing.

519) ATHOL FUGARD, PLAYWRIGHT (South Africa)

Fugard has written benchmark plays, statement plays and wonderful pieces that introduced us to the township. He was responsible for making a lot of people focus on South Africa in a theatrical context. The Road to Mecca affected the political thinking of everyone who saw it. The truthfulness of his writing strikes painfully at the heart. What he has to say makes him an international writer but, first and foremost, it convinces us that he is a great and good man.

520) K'NAAN, RAPPER (Somalia)

A relative newcomer, this Somali rapper made a name in hip hop and world music circles with his inventive 2006 album The Dusty Foot Philosopher. Born in 1978, he spent his formative years trying to avoid Somalia's civil war and listening to hip-hop records sent to him by his father, who was working as a taxi driver in New York. At 13 he moved with his siblings to Harlem, and then on to Rexdale, Ontario, where he became part of a large Somali community and started rapping. A rapid rise ensued, including performing at the 50th anniversary of the UN High Commissioner for Refugees in 2001 and contributing to Youssou N'Dour's album Building Bridges.

521)OUMOU SY, FASHION DESIGNER (Senegal)

The Senegalese designer is known as "Queen of Couture". Her bold avant-garde and Afrocentric fashions are her signature style, with a touch of Western glamour. The 55-year-old Sy is a Renaissance woman; she founded the Dakar Carnival and International Fashion Week and is also a teacher. Elaborate headdresses, vibrant colours, baskets, and even adorning CDs are her trademarks. She has pride for her culture and designs for the modern African woman, who has a bit of a fun side to her.

Historic African Facts

The African continent is widely recognised as the birthplace of humanity and the cradle of civilization. Most notable of African civilisations occurred over 5000 years ago across the Nile valley. The Kemet is also known as Ancient Egypt great achievements. Some of the world's great civilisations can be found in Africa. Civilizations like Kush, Axum, Mali, and Great Zimbabwe flourished in Africa in the years before 1500. It is obvious that European intervention in Africa disrupted and destabilised the African culture and economy.

This section of facts about African is the most important part because it explores the history of Africa. Credit to blackhistorystudies.com this information about the history of Africa.

522) The human race is of African origin. The oldest known skeletal remains of anatomically modern humans (or Homosapiens) were excavated at sites in East Africa. Human remains were discovered at Omo in Ethiopia that was dated at 195,000 years old, the oldest known in the world.

523) Skeletons of pre-humans have been found in Africa that date back between 4 and 5 million years. The oldest known ancestral type of humanity is thought to have been

the Australopithecus ramidus, who lived at least 4.4 million years ago.

524) Africans were the first to organise fishing expeditions 90,000 years ago. At Katanda, a region in north-eastern Zaïre (now Congo), was recovered a finely wrought series of harpoon points, all elaborately polished and barbed. Also uncovered was a tool, equally well crafted, believed to be a dagger. The discoveries suggested the existence of an early aquatic or fishing based culture.

525) Africans were the first to engage in mining 43,000 years ago. In 1964 a hematite mine was found in Swaziland at Bomvu Ridge in the Ngwenya mountain range. Ultimately 300,000 artefacts were recovered including thousands of stone-made mining tools. Adrian Boshier, one of the archaeologists on the site, dated the mine to a staggering 43,200 years old.

526) Africans pioneered basic arithmetic 25,000 years ago. The Ishango bone is a tool handle with notches carved into it found in the Ishango region of Zaïre (now called Congo) near Lake Edward. The bone tool was originally thought to have been over 8,000 years old, but a more sensitive recent dating has given dates of 25,000 years old. On the tool are 3 rows of notches. Row 1 shows three notches carved next to six, four carved next to eight, ten carved next to two fives and finally a seven.

The 3 and 6, 4 and 8, and 10 and 5, represent the process of doubling. Row 2 shows eleven notches carved next to twenty-one notches, and nineteen notches carved next to nine notches. This represents 10 + 1, 20 + 1, 20 – 1 and 10 – 1. Finally, Row 3 shows eleven notches, thirteen notches, seventeen notches and nineteen notches. 11, 13, 17 and 19 are the prime numbers between 10 and 20.

527) Africans cultivated crops 12,000 years ago, the first known advances in agriculture. Professor Fred Wendorf discovered that people in Egypt's Western Desert cultivated crops of barley, capers, chick-peas, dates, legumes, lentils and wheat. Their ancient tools were also recovered. There were grindstones, milling stones, cutting blades, hide scrapers, engraving burins, and mortars and pestles.

528) Africans mummified their dead 9,000 years ago. A mummified infant was found under the Uan Muhuggiag rock shelter in south-western Libya. The infant was buried in the foetal position and was mummified using a very sophisticated technique that must have taken hundreds of years to evolve. The technique predates the earliest mummies known in Ancient Egypt by at least 1,000 years. Carbon dating is controversial but the mummy may date from 7438 (±220) BC.

529) Africans carved the world's first colossal sculpture 7,000 or more years ago. The Great Sphinx of Giza was fashioned with the head of a man combined with the body of a lion. A key and important question raised by this monument was: How old is it? In October 1991 Professor Robert Schoch, a geologist from Boston University, demonstrated that the Sphinx was sculpted between 5000 BC and 7000 BC, dates that he considered conservative.

530) On the 1 March 1979, the New York Times carried an article on its front page also page sixteen that was entitled Nubian Monarchy called Oldest. In this article, we were assured that: "Evidence of the oldest recognizable monarchy in human history, preceding the rise of the earliest Egyptian kings by several generations, has been discovered in artefacts from ancient Nubia" (i.e. the territory of northern Sudan and the southern portion of modern Egypt.)

531) The ancient Egyptians had the same type of tropically adapted skeletal proportions as modern Black Africans. A 2003 paper appeared in American Journal of Physical Anthropology by Dr Sonia Zakrzewski entitled Variation in Ancient Egyptian Stature and Body Proportions where she states that: "The raw values in Table 6 suggest that Egyptians had the 'super-Negroid' body plan described

by Robins (1983). The values for the brachial and crural indices show that the distal segments of each limb are longer relative to the proximal segments than in many 'African' populations."

532) The ancient Egyptians had Afro combs. One writer tells us that the Egyptians "manufactured a very striking range of combs in ivory: the shape of these is distinctly African and is like the combs used even today by Africans and those of African descent."

533) The Funerary Complex in the ancient Egyptian city of Saqqara is the oldest building that tourists regularly visit today. An outer wall, now mostly in ruins, surrounded the whole structure. Through the entrance are a series of columns, the first stone-built columns known to historians. The North House also has ornamental columns built into the walls that have papyrus-like capitals. Also inside the complex is the Ceremonial Court, made of limestone blocks that have been quarried and then shaped. In the centre of the complex is the Step Pyramid, the first of 90 Egyptian pyramids.

534) The first Great Pyramid of Giza, the most extraordinary building in history, was a staggering 481 feet tall – the equivalent of a 40-storey building. It was made of 2.3 million blocks of limestone and granite, some weighing 100 tons.

535) The ancient Egyptian city of Kahun was the world's first planned city. Rectangular and walled, the city was divided into two parts. One part housed the wealthier inhabitants – the scribes, officials and foremen. The other part housed the ordinary people. The streets of the western section, in particular, were straight, laid out on a grid, and crossed each other at right angles. A stone gutter, over half a metre wide, ran down the centre of every street.

536) Egyptian mansions were discovered in Kahun – each boasting 70 rooms, divided into four sections or quarters. There was a master's quarter, quarters for women and servants, quarters for offices and finally, quarters for granaries, each facing a central courtyard. The master's quarters had an open court with a stone water tank for bathing. Surrounding this was a colonnade.

537) The Labyrinth in the Egyptian city of Hawara with its massive layout, multiple courtyards, chambers and halls, was the very largest building in antiquity. Boasting three thousand rooms, 1,500 of them were above ground and the other 1,500 were underground.

538) Toilets and sewerage systems existed in ancient Egypt. One of the pharaohs built a city now known as Amarna. An American urban planner noted that: "Great importance was attached to cleanliness in Amarna as in

other Egyptian cities. Toilets and sewers were in use to dispose of waste. Soap was made for washing the body. Perfumes and essences were popular against body odour. A solution of natron was used to keep insects from houses . . . Amarna may have been the first planned 'garden city'."

539) Sudan has more pyramids than any other country on earth – even more than Egypt. There are at least 223 pyramids in the Sudanese cities of Al Kurru, Nuri, Gebel Barkal and Meroë. They are generally 20 to 30 metres high and steep-sided.

540) The Sudanese city of Meroë is rich in surviving monuments. Becoming the capital of the Kushite Empire between 590 BC until AD 350, there are 84 pyramids in this city alone, many built with their own miniature temple. Also, there are ruins of a bathhouse sharing affinities with those of the Romans. Its central feature is a large pool approached by a flight of steps with waterspouts decorated with lion heads.

541) Bling culture has a long and interesting history. Gold was used to decorate ancient Sudanese temples. One writer reported that: "Recent excavations at Meroe and Mussawwarat es-Sufra revealed temples with walls and statues covered with gold leaf".

542) In around 300 BC, the Sudanese invented a writing script that had twenty-three letters of which four were vowels and there was also a word divider. Hundreds of ancient texts have survived that were in this script. Some are on display in the British Museum.

543) In central Nigeria, West Africa's oldest civilisation flourished between 1000 BC and 300 BC. Discovered in 1928, the ancient culture was called the Nok Civilisation, named after the village in which the early artefacts were discovered. Two modern scholars, declare that "after calibration, the period of Nok art spans from 1000 BC until 300 BC". The site itself is much older going back as early as 4580 or 4290 BC.

544) West Africans built in stone by 1100 BC. In the Tichitt-Walata region of Mauritania, archaeologists have found "large stone masonry villages" that date back to 1100 BC. The villages consisted of roughly circular compounds connected by "well-defined streets".

545) By 250 BC, the foundations of West Africa's oldest cities were established such as Old Djenné in Mali.

546) Kumbi Saleh, the capital of Ancient Ghana, flourished from 300 to 1240 AD. Located in modern-day Mauritania, archaeological excavations have revealed houses, almost habitable today, for want of renovation and several storeys high. They had underground rooms,

staircases and connecting halls. Some had nine rooms. One part of the city alone is estimated to have housed 30,000 people.

547) West Africa had walled towns and cities in the pre-colonial period. Winwood Reade, an English historian visited West Africa in the nineteenth century and commented that: "There are . . . thousands of large walled cities resembling those of Europe in the Middle Ages, or of ancient Greece."

548) Lord Lugard, an English official, estimated in 1904 that there were 170 walled towns still in existence in the whole of just the Kano province of northern Nigeria.

549) Cheques are not quite as new an invention as we were led to believe. In the tenth century, an Arab geographer, Ibn Haukal, visited a fringe region of Ancient Ghana. Writing in 951 AD, he told of a cheque for 42,000 golden dinars written to a merchant in the city of Audoghast by his partner in Sidjilmessa.

550) Ibn Haukal, writing in 951 AD, informs us that the King of Ghana was "the richest king on the face of the earth" whose pre-eminence was due to the quantity of gold nuggets that had been amassed by himself and by his predecessors.

551) The Nigerian city of Ile-Ife was paved in 1000 AD on the orders of a female ruler with decorations that originated

in Ancient America. Naturally, no-one wants to explain how this took place approximately 500 years before the time of Christopher Columbus!

552) West Africa had bling culture in 1067 AD. One source mentions that when the Emperor of Ghana gives audience to his people: "he sits in a pavilion around which stand his horses caparisoned in cloth of gold: behind him stand ten pages holding shields and gold-mounted swords: and on his right hand are the sons of the princes of his empire, splendidly clad and with gold plaited into their hair . . . The gate of the chamber is guarded by dogs of an excellent breed . . . they wear collars of gold and silver."

553) Glass windows existed at that time. The residence of the Ghanaian Emperor in 1116 AD was: "A well-built castle, thoroughly fortified, decorated inside with sculptures and pictures, and having glass windows."

554) The Grand Mosque in the Malian city of Djenné, described as "the largest adobe [clay] building in the world", was first raised in 1204 AD. It was built on a square plan where each side is 56 metres in length. It has three large towers on one side, each with projecting wooden buttresses.

555) One of the great achievements of the Yoruba was their urban culture. "By the year A.D. 1300," says a modern scholar, "the Yoruba people built numerous walled cities

surrounded by farms". The cities were Owu, Oyo, Ijebu, Ijesa, Ketu, Popo, Egba, Sabe, Dassa, Egbado, Igbomina, the sixteen Ekiti principalities, Owo and Ondo.

556) Yoruba metal art of the mediaeval period was of world-class. One scholar wrote that Yoruba art "would stand comparison with anything which Ancient Egypt, Classical Greece and Rome, or Renaissance Europe had to offer."

557) In the Malian city of Gao stands the Mausoleum of Askia the Great, a weird sixteenth-century edifice that resembles a step pyramid.

558) Thousands of mediaeval tumuli have been found across West Africa. Nearly 7,000 were discovered in north-west Senegal alone spread over nearly 1,500 sites. They were probably built between 1000 and 1300 AD.

559) Excavations at the Malian city of Gao carried out by Cambridge University revealed glass windows. One of the finds was entitled: "Fragments of alabaster window surrounds and a piece of pink window glass, Gao 10th – 14th century."

560) In 1999 the BBC produced a television series entitled Millennium. The programme devoted to the fourteenth century opens with the following disclosure: "In the fourteenth century, the century of the scythe, natural disasters threatened civilisations with extinction. The

Black Death kills more people in Europe, Asia and North Africa than any catastrophe has before. Civilisations which avoid the plague thrive. In West Africa, the Empire of Mali becomes the richest in the world."

561) Malian sailors got to America in 1311 AD, 181 years before Columbus. An Egyptian scholar, Ibn Fadl Al-Umari, published on this sometime around 1342. In the tenth chapter of his book, there is an account of two large maritime voyages ordered by the predecessor of Mansa Musa, a king who inherited the Malian throne in 1312. This mariner king is not named by Al-Umari, but modern writers identify him as Mansa Abubakari II.

562) On a pilgrimage to Mecca in 1324 AD, a Malian ruler, Mansa Musa, brought so much money with him that his visit resulted in the collapse of gold prices in Egypt and Arabia. It took twelve years for the economies of the region to normalise.

563) West African gold mining took place on a vast scale. One modern writer said: "It is estimated that the total amount of gold mined in West Africa up to 1500 was 3,500 tons, worth more than $30 billion in today's market."

564) The old Malian capital of Niani had a 14th-century building called the Hall of Audience. It was surmounted by a dome, adorned with arabesques of striking colours.

The windows of an upper floor were plated with wood and framed in silver; those of a lower floor were plated with wood, framed in gold.

565) Mali in the 14th century was highly urbanised. Sergio Domian, an Italian art and architecture scholar, wrote the following about this period: "Thus was laid the foundation of an urban civilisation. At the height of its power, Mali had at least 400 cities, and the interior of the Niger Delta was very densely populated".

566) The Malian city of Timbuktu had a 14th-century population of 115,000 – 5 times larger than mediaeval London. Mansa Musa built the Djinguerebere Mosque in the fourteenth century. There was the University Mosque in which 25,000 students studied and the Oratory of Sidi Yayia. There were over 150 Koran schools in which 20,000 children were instructed. London, by contrast, had a total 14th-century population of 20,000 people.

567) National Geographic recently described Timbuktu as the Paris of the mediaeval world, on account of its intellectual culture. According to Professor Henry Louis Gates, 25,000 university students studied there.

568) Many old West African families have private library collections that go back hundreds of years. The Mauritanian cities of Chinguetti and Oudane have a total of 3,450 hands written mediaeval books. There may be

another 6,000 books still surviving in the other city of Walata. Some date back to the 8th century AD. There are 11,000 books in private collections in Niger. Finally, in Timbuktu, Mali, there are about 700,000 surviving books.

569) A collection of one thousand six hundred books was considered a small library for a West African scholar of the 16th century. Professor Ahmed Baba of Timbuktu is recorded as saying that he had the smallest library of any of his friends – he had only 1600 volumes.

570) Concerning these old manuscripts, Michael Palin, in his TV series Sahara, said the imam of Timbuktu "has a collection of scientific texts that clearly show the planets circling the sun. They date back hundreds of years . . . Its convincing evidence that the scholars of Timbuktu knew a lot more than their counterparts in Europe. In the fifteenth century in Timbuktu, the mathematicians knew about the rotation of the planets, knew about the details of the eclipse, they knew things which we had to wait for 150 almost 200 years to know in Europe when Galileo and Copernicus came up with these same calculations and were given a very hard time for it."

571)The Songhai Empire of 16th century West Africa had a government position called Minister for Etiquette and Protocol.

572) The mediaeval Nigerian city of Benin was built to "a scale comparable with the Great Wall of China". There was a vast system of defensive walling totalling 10,000 miles in all. Even before the full extent of the city walling had become apparent the Guinness Book of Records carried an entry in the 1974 edition that described the city as: "The largest earthworks in the world carried out before the mechanical era."

573) Benin art of the Middle Ages was of the highest quality. An official of the Berlin Museum für Völkerkunde once stated that: "These works from Benin are equal to the very finest examples of European casting technique. Benvenuto Cellini could not have cast them better, nor could anyone else before or after him... Technically; these bronzes represent the very highest possible achievement."

574) Winwood Reade described his visit to the Ashanti Royal Palace of Kumasi in 1874: "We went to the king's palace, which consists of many courtyards, each surrounded with alcoves and verandahs, and having two gates or doors so that each yard was a thoroughfare . . . But the part of the palace fronting the street was a stone house, Moorish in its style . . . with a flat roof and a parapet, and suites of apartments on the first floor. It was built by Fanti masons many years ago. The rooms

upstairs remind me of Wardour Street. Each was a perfect Old Curiosity Shop. Books in many languages, Bohemian glass, clocks, silver plate, old furniture, Persian rugs, Kidderminster carpets, pictures and engravings, numberless chests and coffers. A sword bearing the inscription From Queen Victoria to the King of Ashantee. A copy of the Times, 17 October 1843. With these were many specimens of Moorish and Ashanti handicraft."

575) In the mid-nineteenth century, William Clarke, an English visitor to Nigeria, remarked that: "As good an article of cloth can be woven by the Yoruba weavers as by any people . . . in durability, their cloths far excel the prints and homespuns of Manchester."

576) The recently discovered 9th-century Nigerian city of Eredo was found to be surrounded by a wall that was 100 miles long and seventy feet high in places. The internal area was a staggering 400 square miles.

577) On the subject of cloth, Kongolese textiles were also distinguished. Various European writers of the sixteenth and seventeenth centuries wrote of the delicate crafts of the peoples living in eastern Kongo and adjacent regions who manufactured damasks, sarcenets, satins, taffeta, cloth of tissue and velvet. Professor DeGraft-Johnson made the curious observation that: "Their brocades, both high and low, were far more valuable than the Italian."

578) On Kongolese metallurgy of the Middle Ages, one modern scholar wrote that: "There is no doubting . . . the existence of an expert metallurgical art in the ancient Kongo… The Bakongo were aware of the toxicity of lead vapours. They devised preventative and curative methods, both pharmacological (massive doses of pawpaw and palm oil) and mechanical (exerting of pressure to free the digestive tract), for combating lead poisoning."

579) In Nigeria, the royal palace in the city of Kano dates back to the fifteenth century. Begun by Muhammad Rumfa (ruled 1463-99) it has gradually evolved over generations into a very imposing complex. A colonial report of the city from 1902, described it as "a network of buildings covering an area of 33 acres and surrounded by a wall 20 to 30 feet high outside and 15 feet inside… in itself no mean citadel".

580) A sixteenth-century traveller visited the central African civilisation of Kanem-Borno and commented that the emperor's cavalry had golden "stirrups, spurs, bits and buckles." Even the ruler's dogs had "chains of the finest gold".

581) One of the government positions in mediaeval Kanem-Borno was Astronomer Royal.

582) Ngazargamu, the capital city of Kanem-Borno, became one of the largest cities in the seventeenth-century world. By 1658 AD, the metropolis, according to an architectural scholar housed "about a quarter of a million people". It had 660 streets. Many were wide and unbending, reflective of town planning.

583) The Nigerian city of Surame flourished in the sixteenth century. Even in ruin, it was an impressive sight, built on a horizontal vertical grid. A modern scholar describes it thus: "The walls of Surame are about 10 miles in circumference and include many large bastions or walled suburbs running out at right angles to the main wall. The large compound at Kanta is still visible in the centre, with ruins of many buildings, one of which is said to have been two-storied. The striking feature of the walls and whole ruins is the extensive use of stone and tsokuwa (laterite gravel) or very hard red building mud, evidently brought from a distance. There is a big mound of this near the north gate about 8 feet in height. The walls show regular courses of masonry to a height of 20 feet and more in several places. The best-preserved portion is that known as sirati (the bridge) a little north of the eastern gate . . . The main city walls here appears to have provided a very strongly guarded entrance about 30 feet wide."

584) The Nigerian city of Kano in 1851 produced an estimated 10 million pairs of sandals and 5 million hides each year for export.

585) In 1246 AD Dunama II of Kanem-Borno exchanged embassies with Al-Mustansir, the king of Tunis. He sent the North African court a costly present, which apparently included a giraffe. An old chronicle noted that the rare animal "created a sensation in Tunis".

586) By the third century BC, the city of Carthage on the coast of Tunisia was opulent and impressive. It had a population of 700,000 and may even have approached a million. Lining both sides of three streets were rows of tall houses six storeys high.

587) The Ethiopian city of Axum has a series of 7 giant obelisks that date from perhaps 300 BC to 300 AD. They have details carved into them that represent windows and doorways of several storeys. The largest obelisk, now fallen, is in fact "the largest monolith ever made anywhere in the world". It is 108 feet long, weighs a staggering 500 tons, and represents a thirteen-storey building.

588) Ethiopia minted its own coins over 1,500 years ago. One scholar wrote that: "Almost no other contemporary state anywhere in the world could issue in gold, a

statement of sovereignty achieved only by Rome, Persia, and the Kushan kingdom in northern India at the time."

589) The Ethiopian script of the 4th century AD influenced the writing script of Armenia. A Russian historian noted that: "Soon after its creation, the Ethiopic vocalised script began to influence the scripts of Armenia and Georgia. D. A. Olderogge suggested that Mesrop Mashtotz used the vocalised Ethiopic script when he invented the Armenian alphabet."

590) "In the first half of the first millennium CE," says a modern scholar, Ethiopia "was ranked as one of the world's greatest empires". A Persian cleric of the third century AD identified it as the third most important state in the world after Persia and Rome.

591) Ethiopia has 11 underground mediaeval churches built by being carved out of the ground. In the twelfth and thirteenth centuries AD, Roha became the new capital of the Ethiopians. Conceived as a New Jerusalem by its founder, Emperor Lalibela (c.1150-1230), it contains 11 churches, all carved out of the rock of the mountains by hammer and chisel. All of the temples were carved to a depth of 11 metres or so below ground level. The largest is the House of the Redeemer, a staggering 33.7 metres long, 23.7 metres wide and 11.5 metres deep.

592) Lalibela is not the only place in Ethiopia to have such wonders. A contemporary archaeologist reports research that was conducted in the region in the early 1970s when: "startling numbers of churches built in caves or partially or completely cut from the living rock were revealed not only in Tigre and Lalibela but as far south as Addis Ababa. Soon at least 1,500 were known. At least as many more probably await revelation."

593) In 1209 AD Emperor Lalibela of Ethiopia sent an embassy to Cairo bringing the sultan unusual gifts including an elephant, a hyena, a zebra, and a giraffe.

594) In Southern Africa, there are at least 600 stone built ruins in the regions of Zimbabwe, Mozambique and South Africa. These ruins are called Mazimbabwe in Shona, the Bantu language of the builders, and means great revered house and "signifies court".

595) Great Zimbabwe was the largest of these ruins. It consists of 12 clusters of buildings, spread over 3 square miles. Its outer walls were made from 100,000 tons of granite bricks. In the fourteenth century, the city housed 18,000 people, comparable in size to that of London of the same period.

596) Bling culture existed in this region. At the time of our last visit, the Horniman Museum in London had exhibits of headrests with the caption: "Headrests have been used

in Africa since the time of the Egyptian pharaohs. Remains of some headrests, once covered in gold foil, have been found in the ruins of Great Zimbabwe and burial sites like Mapungubwe dating to the twelfth century after Christ."

597) Dr Albert Churchward, the author of Signs and Symbols of Primordial Man, pointed out that writing was found in one of the stone-built ruins: "Lt.-Col. E. L. de Cordes . . . who was in South Africa for three years, informed the writer that in one of the 'Ruins' there is a 'stone-chamber,' with a vast quantity of Papyri, covered with old Egyptian hieroglyphics. A Boer hunter discovered this, and a large quantity was used to light a fire with, and yet still a larger quantity remained there now."

598) On bling culture, one seventeenth-century visitor to southern African empire of Monomotapa, that ruled over this vast region, wrote that: "The people dress in various ways: at the court of the Kings their grandees wear cloths of rich silk, damask, satin, gold and silk cloth; these are three widths of satin, each width four covados [2.64m], each sewn to the next, sometimes with gold lace in between, trimmed on two sides, like a carpet, with a gold and silk fringe, sewn in place with a two fingers' wide ribbon, woven with gold roses on silk."

599) Southern Africans mined gold on an epic scale. One modern writer tells us that: "The estimated amount of gold ore mined from the entire region by the ancients was staggering, exceeding 43 million tons. The ore yielded nearly 700 tons of pure gold which today would be valued at over $7.5 billion."

600) Apparently, the Monomotapan royal palace at Mount Fura had chandeliers hanging from the ceiling. An eighteenth-century geography book provided the following data: "The inside consists of a great variety of sumptuous apartments, spacious and lofty halls, all adorned with a magnificent cotton tapestry, the manufacture of the country. The floors, ceilings, beams and rafters are all either gilt or plated with gold curiously wrought, as are also the chairs of state, tables, benches &c. The candle-sticks and branches are made of ivory inlaid with gold, and hang from the ceiling by chains of the same metal, or of silver gilt."

601) Monomotapa had a social welfare system. Antonio Bocarro, a Portuguese contemporary, informs us that the Emperor: "shows great charity to the blind and maimed, for these are called the king's poor, and have land and revenues for their subsistence, and when they wish to pass through the kingdoms, wherever they come food and drinks are given to them at the public cost as long as they

remain there, and when they leave that place to go to another they are provided with what is necessary for their journey, and a guide, and someone to carry their wallet to the next village. In every place where they come there is the same obligation."

602) Many southern Africans have indigenous and pre-colonial words for 'gun'. Scholars have generally been reluctant to investigate or explain this fact.

603) Evidence discovered in 1978 showed that East Africans were making steel for more than 1,500 years: "Assistant Professor of Anthropology Peter Schmidt and Professor of Engineering Donald H. Avery have found as long as 2,000 years ago Africans living on the western shores of Lake Victoria had produced carbon steel in preheated forced draft furnaces, a method that was technologically more sophisticated than any developed in Europe until the mid-nineteenth century."

604) Ruins of a 300 BC astronomical observatory were found at Namoratunga in Kenya. Africans were mapping the movements of stars such as Triangulum, Aldebaran, Bellatrix, Central Orion, etcetera, as well as the moon, to create a lunar calendar of 354 days.

605) Autopsies and caesarean operations were routinely and effectively carried out by surgeons in pre-colonial Uganda. The surgeons routinely used antiseptics,

anaesthetics and cautery iron. Commenting on a Ugandan caesarean operation that appeared in the Edinburgh Medical Journal in 1884, one author wrote: "The whole conduct of the operation . . . suggests a skilled long-practised surgical team at work conducting a well-tried and familiar operation with smooth efficiency."

606) Sudan in the mediaeval period had churches, cathedrals, monasteries and castles. Their ruins still exist today.

607) The mediaeval Nubian Kingdoms kept archives. From the site of Qasr Ibrim legal texts, documents and correspondence were discovered. An archaeologist informs us that: "On the site are preserved thousands of documents in Meroitic, Latin, Greek, Coptic, Old Nubian, Arabic and Turkish."

608) Glass windows existed in mediaeval Sudan. Archaeologists found evidence of window glass at the Sudanese cities of Old Dongola and Hambukol.

609) Bling culture existed in mediaeval Sudan. Archaeologists found an individual buried at the Monastery of the Holy Trinity in the city of Old Dongola. He was clad in an extremely elaborate garb consisting of costly textiles of various fabrics including gold thread. At the city of Soba East, there were individuals buried in fine clothing, including items with golden thread.

610) Style and fashion existed in mediaeval Sudan. A dignitary at Jebel Adda in the late thirteenth century AD was interned with a long coat of red and yellow patterned damask folded over his body. Underneath, he wore plain cotton trousers of long and baggy cut. A pair of red leather slippers with turned-up toes lay at the foot of the coffin. The body was wrapped in enormous pieces of gold brocaded striped silk.

611) Sudan in the ninth century AD had housing complexes with bathrooms and piped water. An archaeologist wrote that Old Dongola, the capital of Makuria, had: a[n] . . . eighth to . . . ninth century housing complex. The houses discovered here differ in their hitherto unencountered spatial layout as well as their functional programme (water supply installation, bathroom with heating system) and interiors decorated with murals."

612) In 619 AD, the Nubians sent a gift of a giraffe to the Persians.

613) The East Coast, from Somalia to Mozambique, has ruins of well over 50 towns and cities. They flourished from the ninth to the sixteenth centuries AD.

614) Chinese records of the fifteenth century AD note that Mogadishu had houses of "four or five storeys high".

615) Gedi, near the coast of Kenya, is one of the East African ghost towns. Its ruins, dating from the fourteenth

or fifteenth centuries, include the city walls, the palace, private houses, the Great Mosque, seven smaller mosques, and three pillar tombs.

616) The ruined mosque in the Kenyan city of Gedi had a water purifier made of limestone for recycling water.

617) The palace in the Kenyan city of Gedi contains evidence of piped water controlled by taps. In addition, it had bathrooms and indoor toilets.

618) A visitor in 1331 AD considered the Tanzanian city of Kilwa to be of world-class. He wrote that it was the "principal city on the coast the greater part of whose inhabitants are Zanj of very black complexion." Later on, he says: "Kilwa is one of the most beautiful and well-constructed cities in the world. The whole of it is elegantly built."

619) Bling culture existed in early Tanzania. A Portuguese chronicler of the sixteenth century wrote that: "They are finely clad in many rich garments of gold and silk and cotton, and the women as well; also with many gold and silver chains and bracelets, which they wear on their legs and arms, and many jewelled earrings in their ears".

620) In 1961 a British archaeologist, found the ruins of Husuni Kubwa, the royal palace of the Tanzanian city of Kilwa. It had over a hundred rooms, including a reception

hall, galleries, courtyards, terraces and an octagonal swimming pool.

621) In 1414 the Kenyan city of Malindi sent ambassadors to China carrying a gift that created a sensation at the Imperial Court. It was, of course, a giraffe.

Ancient African Kingdoms and Empires

622) Zulu Kingdom

One of the greater kingdoms of southern Africa, the Zulu Kingdom encompassed much of what is now KwaZulu-Natal in South Africa. Some may have heard of Shaka Zulu, the prominent leader of the Zulus born in 1787. A brilliant tactician, he instituted many militaries, social, cultural, and political reforms before eventually losing his grip on his people and mind. He was assassinated in 1828. By the 1870s, British forces fought a war with the Zulus and won, despite early losses.

623) Kingdom of Kongo

Existing as an independent and powerful kingdom for almost 500 years, the Kingdom of Kongo stretched from northern Angola to Gabon, encompassing much of the Atlantic coast in west-central Africa and influenced nearby inland groups. The Kongo had a highly structured army that, at times, was up to 70,000 strong. Their political and economic structures were complex and their currency was made from shells known as nzimbu.

624) Axumite Empire

The Axumite Empire existed for nearly 1,000 years (from shortly after the birth of Christ to 940 AD). At the crossroads of many transcontinental trade routes, Axum controlled what is now Eritrea and northern Ethiopia on the Red Sea Coast. Eventually subjugating parts of Sudan and Arabia, the Axumites created their own alphabet, Ge'ez which is the syllabary of Ethiopia, erected monolithic obelisks which still stand today, and even had a feudal system with slaves.

625) Kingdom of Kush

Coexisting in the later era of Ancient Egypt, the Kingdom of Kush was centred around the Upper Nile, in modern-day Sudan, stretching a few hundred miles north and south of the confluence of the Blue and White branches (present-day Khartoum). The Nile in Sudan is littered with ancient temples, pyramids, and tombs. Some scholars have argued that the Kushite culture was one and the same with Egypt, but they do have differences. The Nubian kings/pharaohs were black and even subjugated Egypt for a brief period of time.

626) Songhai Empire

Once the largest empire in West Africa, Songhai peaked in the 1500s and 1600s. Centered around Gao and the Niger River in Mali, the empire grew and absorbed neighbouring states, becoming one of the largest Islamic states in Africa. Timbuktu and its environs became the centre of not only trade but learning in the entire region. Culturally, the Songhai had an extensive clan and guild structure, but the empire fell into decline after wars of succession and a Moroccan invasion.

627) Abyssinian Empire

The great Abyssinian or Ethiopian Empire proudly stood from 1137 until 1974, one of the only empires in Africa to last until the late 20th century — many famous rulers included names like Yohannes, Tewodros, Menelik, and Halie Selassie. Most notably, the empire had a strong military that defeated multiple invaders over the centuries including the Italians, leaving Ethiopia with the distinction of the only country in Africa to never fall under the colonial influence.

628) The Land of Punt

Few African civilizations are as mysterious as Punt. Historical accounts of the kingdom date to around 2500

B.C., when it appears in Egyptian records as a "Land of the Gods" rich in ebony, gold, myrrh and exotic animals such as apes and leopards. The Egyptians are known to have sent huge caravans and flotillas on trade missions to Punt—most notably during the 15th century B.C. reign of Queen Hatshepsut—yet they never identified where it was located. The site of the fabled kingdom is now a hotly debated topic among scholars. The Arabian Peninsula and the Levant have both been proposed as potential candidates, but most believe it existed somewhere on the Red Sea coast of East Africa.

629) The Mali Empire

The founding of the Mali Empire dates to the 1200s, when a ruler named Sundiata Keita—sometimes called the "Lion King"—led a revolt against a Sosso king and united his subjects into a new state. Under Keita and his successors, the empire tightened its grip over a large portion of West Africa and grew rich on trade. Its most important cities were Djenné and Timbuktu, both of which were renowned for their elaborate adobe mosques and Islamic schools. One such institution, Timbuktu's Sankore University, included a library with an estimated 700,000 manuscripts. One legendary tale about the kingdom's riches concerns the ruler Mansa Musa, who made a stopover in Egypt during a 14th century pilgrimage to Mecca. According to contemporary sources, Musa dished out so much gold during the visit that he caused its value to plummet in Egyptian markets for several years.

630) Carthaginian Empire

Lasting a millennium, the Carthaginian Empire controlled most of North Africa, and parts of what is now Spain, Italy, and France at various times. Based around the Phoenician city-state of Carthage (present-day Tunis), Carthage was known for perpetually fighting wars. Its most brilliant leader and military mind being Hannibal, known for leading his army including war elephants through Europe and across the Alps in a failed attempt to sack Rome by land.

631) Great Zimbabwe

Great Zimbabwe was created out of the Kingdom of Mapungubwe in the 1200s. The new Kingdom of Zimbabwe built upon the masonic and artistic traditions of Mapungubwe. A three-tiered class system was established as well as taxation, trade, and over 150 "minor Zimbabwe's." Eventually falling into decline within a few hundred years, the ruins of Great Zimbabwe were some of the largest stone structures in Africa.

632) Dynastic Egypt

Beginning in 3150 BC with political unification under the first pharaoh, Egypt had the longest and most well-known empire in history. Its technological, cultural, linguistic, economic, social, and artistic innovations are without parallel in the course of human history. Volumes have been written about its accomplishments and that of its leaders, we won't bore you, so look up the rest yourself.

633) Sokoto Caliphate

Founded during the Fulani War in 1809, the Sokoto Caliphate was the most powerful entity in West Africa in the 19th century. Administered as an Islamic Caliphate with smaller vassal emirates paying tribute to the sultan, it was eventually subjugated by the British a century later; however, the Sultan of Sokoto still exists as a position and is revered by millions of Muslims in northern Nigeria.

634) Kingdom of Jolof

From 1549 until 1875, the Kingdom of Jolof (Wolof) was a powerful kingdom in what is now Senegal and Gambia.

The Islamic monarchy existed as a confederacy, with smaller states joining under the rule of Jolof and paying tribute. In 1875, the theocratic Imamate of Futa Jallon brought jihad upon its neighbour; the kingdom never recovered and the French took over soon thereafter. C'est la vie. The next time you eat Jollof rice, you can thank this kingdom.

635) Sultante of Darfur

What's the old adage about not learning from history? Sudan has a myriad of problems we won't get into here. A fairly large one though is Darfur. That's because, like (the newly independent) South Sudan, Darfur (literally "realm of the Fur") was its own sultanate for centuries. Encompassing the Jebel Marrah Mountains straddling the border between Sudan and Chad, the sultanate was abolished by the British (no surprise) and brought into Anglo-Egyptian Sudan in 1916.

636) Kingdom of Dahomey

The Kingdom of Dahomey was possibly the most important power on the Atlantic Coast of West Africa from 1600 – 1900. Dahomey (now known as Benin) was crucial in the slave trade, supplying upwards of 20% of the unfortunate Africans who would be shipped to the

New World. The kingdom was highly organized, from trade with Europe to administration and taxes to an orderly military. Known for their corps of female warriors called Amazons, the French finally defeated the last ruler "King Shark Behanzin" in 1894.

637) Ashanti Union

From 1670 until 1902, the Ashanti Union was one of the most modern states in Africa and stretched from its borders with Dahomey (Benin) to what is now the Ivory Coast. One of the most studied empires in Africa, their highly organized military was effective because of the excellent strategy and early adoption of European firearms into their ranks. Trade, art, culture, and more all flourished during the Union which became Ghana.

638) The Ghana Empire (c. 300 until c. 1100)

Properly known as Wagadou (Ghana being the title of its ruler), was a West African empire located in the area of present-day southeastern Mauritania and western Mali. Complex societies based on trans-Saharan trade in salt and gold had existed in the region since ancient times, but the introduction of the camel to the western Sahara in the 3rd century CE, opened the way to great changes in the area that became the Ghana Empire.

639) Buganda Kingdom

The Buganda Kingdom which was established in the 1300s is one of the rare kingdoms that still exist in Africa (although as a subnational entity). However, the Baganda make up the largest ethnic group of Uganda at 17%. The family unit and male lineage are what dictates social customs. Disestablished by Milton Obote in the 1960s, the re-establishment of the king was implemented in 1993, although sadly, the royal Kasubi Tombs which housed the last four kings were destroyed by arson in 2010.

Ancient African Kings

640) Mansa Kankan MusaMansa Musa ruled the Kingdom of Mali from 1306 A.D. to 1332 A.D. During 1324, Musa travelled to Mecca along with 72,000 residents from the city of Timbuktu for a holy pilgrimage. Under Musa's leadership, The Kingdom of Mali became one of the richest empires in the world.

641) Sunni Ali Sunni Ali is the founder of the Songhai Empire. During his reign, the Songhai Kingdom reached its peak by surpassing the Empire of Mali and absorbing its territories including the city of Timbuktu. It was also during his time that Islam spread across both urban and rural centres. According to scholars; Sunni Ali had a brilliant military mind. As a matter of fact, he had amphibious forces that were often patrolling and attacking in the Niger River.

642) Amenhotep III Amenhotep III was considered as one of the greatest Pharaohs of Egypt. It was during his reign that Egypt enjoyed stability, wealth, and peace and developed a noticeable influence in diplomacy and foreign policy. Pharaoh Amenhotep III also built monuments, buildings, and other projects. In fact, Amenhotep constructed the first human-made lake

outside his palace in Malkata to honour his wife, Queen Tiye. Several proofs of this can be seen on the Amarna letters that are coming from Babylon, Hatti, Mitanni, and Assyria.

643) Sundiata Keita was the founder of Ancient Mali Empire. He is also widely known as the Prince of the Mandinka people. His rise to fame is detailed in the poem called The Epic of Sundiata which was written and told by the Griots. The poem chronicles the fabled origins of Sundiata and tells his pre-ordained rise to power, the start of the Mali Empire, and his imperial conquests. During his reign, Sundiata conquered all the territories that are now located in the present-day Guinea Bissau, Senegal, and The Gambia. The dynastic line he came from subsequently became one of the richest and the most overpowering ancient West African empires.

644) Shaka Zulu Shaka Zulu became the King of Zulu in South Africa from 1818 to 1828. He is best remembered for turning Zulu fighters to great warriors. All of his troops used standardized weapons to combat their enemies.

645) Oba Oduduwa – Oyo Empire (Yoruba land, Nigeria) around 700 - Oduduwa is considered the progenitor of the Yoruba land and Yoruba Dynasty. He is a national folk-hero and considered a primordial God in Yoruba culture.

There is much debate on where Oduduwa originally came from or when exactly he founded the Yoruba land and language; however, he and his clan descended on the lower region of Nigeria and defeated several existing settlements to establish Yoruba land. Legend has it that he had 16 sons and daughters, and before he died, he sent each one to the centres of his conquered territories to rule autonomously, where they founded the kingdoms of Ila Orangun, Owu, Ketu, Sabe, Popo and Oyo. Oranmiyan thus established the Yoruba dynastic family line.

646) Osei Kofi Tutu 1660 – 1717 Ashanti Kingdom (Ghana) The Ashanti was a highly political, wealthy, and powerful West African Kingdom. The Ashanti was one of the first Sub-Saharan militaries to adopt firearms into their arsenal. Their source of wealth came from the large salt and gold deposits mined in their region, which they traded within the continental African states' trade routes. The Ashanti were an organized and disciplined Akan people. The Akan was the ethnic/linguistic grouping of people who spoke Akan or Twi. There were several Akan States. In 1701 Osei Kofi Tutu, chief of the small Akan city-state of Kumasi helped form the Ashanti Empire by unifying other Akan groups under the Golden Stool (Ashanti Seat of Power). He influenced the other Akan to overthrow the dominating Akan group, the Denkyera, as

well as conquer several other neighbouring states. As the Ashanti, the unified Akan people absorbed several Akan territories and expanded the Ashanti wealth, power and influence. The Golden Stool would remain the seat of power for the Ashanti until the British Imperial Government demanded the sovereignty of the Ashanti be turned over to Britain as its "protectorate." This resulted in the "War of the Golden Stool."

647) Oba Ewuare (also Ewuare the Great) Benin Empire (Edo, Nigeria) 1440 -1473. Oba Ewuare is known as the first king of the Benin Empire, the reformer of Benin City and one of the first warrior kings of West Africa. It's chronicled that during his reign; he conquered and absorbed at least 201 surrounding towns and villages. Together, Ewuare and his son and successor, Oba Ozolua, were responsible for establishing a viable foreign trade in Benin, building substantial palaces and creating several strategic policies, one of which removed the conquered town's chieftains from absolute power but allowed them power in a congressional committee. He also created a patrimonial bureaucracy in which freemen served as military and administrative chiefs. Outside of war and politics, Ewuare is described as a charismatic leader. He established several cultural traditions,

communal events and festivals. Under Ewuare, the tradition of Beninese arts flourished.

648) Taharqa (Egypt & Nubia) 25th Dynasty Reign 690 – 664 BCE. Taharqa was one of the Great Napatan Nubian kings/Pharaohs. After his father, Piye, successfully conquered Egypt in battle, Taharqa united the two kingdoms to form the largest African empire at the time. His empire spanned from the 5th Nile Cataract in Nubia, throughout all of Egypt, up into the Middle East in Palestine. Taharqa is credited with bringing new peace and stability to Egypt, resuming building projects and arts in Egypt and Nubia, which were lost for centuries, at the time.

649) Ezana Axum (Ethiopia) 333 – c. 356. Ezana is celebrated as the First Ethiopian King to embrace Christianity and convert his entire kingdom. He helped establish the Ethiopic Church. He is also credited with bringing the powerful rival kingdom of Meroe (Nubia) to an end. Under his rule, the Axumite kingdom flourished. Under his reign, several unique structures and obelisks were erected. International trade was also increased. His coinage has been unearthed in locations like India and Greece.

650) Endubis 270ce. -300ce Axum (Ethiopia) Axum was a powerful North-East African Empire which rose to power

after the decline of Ancient Egypt and Nubia. Axum is credited with conquering and bringing the ultimate end of the Kingdom of ancient Meroe (Nubia). Axum controlled the horn of Africa across the Red Sea into the Arabian plateau. Endubis was the first king of Ancient Africa to mint coinage, and following Endubis, all Axumite (Ethiopian) Emperors minted their own coinage: gold, silver and bronze pieces with their faces and motto.

Some Of The Best African Footballers Of All Time

651) **SAMUEL ETO'O** - No doubt about our number one. No footballer from African soil can boast of being greater than the Cameroon legend Samuel Eto'o. Alongside Yaya Toure, he won four African Player of the Year Awards. He won Olympic Gold in 2000 before helping Cameroon seal the AFCON title on two other occasions. He scored 130 goals for Barcelona where he won the treble in the 2008-2009 season. He bagged two UEFA Champions League titles for Barca scoring in both finals. He also won the UCL with Inter Milan in 2010 as well as the FIFA Club World Cup. He made both UEFA and FIFA Teams of the Year twice and was third in the 2005 edition of FIFA World's best player award. He has a ton of individual awards to his name and played for a great number of top clubs. He's truly the greatest.

652) **GEORGE WEAH (LIBERIA)** - This guy is the only African footballer to win the Ballon d'Or and the FIFA World Player of the Year after securing both in 1995. He also bagged African Player of the Year on three occasions. He helped PSG win the League title in 1994

before winning two Seria A crowns with AC Milan where he had his most successful spell. Weah scored over 200 goals in his professional career. He's a huge national hero and is now the President of his nation Liberia. What a man!

653) **DIDIER DROGBA (IVORY COAST)** - A predator in the box. One of Premier League's greatest strikers ever and definitely a Chelsea Legend. Named African Player of the Year twice and finished top three an astonishing 8 times. Drogba netted over 300 goals in his professional career and won four Premier League titles, four FA Cup, three English League Cups, two Community Shields and one UEFA Champions League title. He's won the Premier League golden boot and made the Premier League team of the year twice.

654) **ROGER MILLA (CAMEROON)** - Many will say he's the greatest African Player and that's a valid argument. He was a beast. Roger Milla netted 438 goals in 794 matches in his professional career. He won the African Player of the Year award twice and also won the Nation's cup twice for Cameroon. He made World Cup all-star team and was the third-highest goalscorer in 1990. At 42, Milla became the oldest player ever to play in a World Cup final in 1994.

655) **YAYA TOURE (IVORY COAST)** - Not much word needs to be said about Yaya Toure. The Midfielder could star anywhere on the pitch, this was why he had a successful period at the top level. He's easily the best midfielder Africa ever produced. He won absolutely everything there is to win while at Barca, and then joined Man City where he played a crucial role in giving them the League title. His strength, vision and goal-scoring instinct are unmatched. He's the player with the most African Player of the Year award wins with four honours to his name. A true great.

656) **NWANKWO KANU (NIGERIA)** - A legend! This man won almost everything and is one of the few players to have won the UEFA Champions League, English Premier League, FA Cup, Olympic Gold medal and UEFA Cup. He also won the Holland Eredivisie at Ajax thrice and was named African Player of the year twice. He's the greatest Nigerian player of all time and a legend for Arsenal and Ajax as well as Portsmouth.

657) **JAY-JAY OKOCHA (NIGERIA)** - When it comes to pure talent and trickery, no one comes close to Jay-Jay, so good he was named twice. He could dribble an entire team and was a regular in all teams he played for. He won the African Cup of Nations and Olympic Gold with

his nation and had numerous individual awards including two BBC African Player of the Year Awards.

658) **ESSAM EL-HADARY (EGYPT)** - He's definitely the greatest goalkeeper Africa produced. El-Hadary won the African Cup of Nations on four occasions, no other player has more. He made the team of the tournament on three occasions and kept a clean sheet in three AFCON finals. He won eight League titles with Al-Merreikh and Al-Ahly. He played 22 years for the Egypt national team, a national hero.

659) **SEYDOU KEITA (MALI)** - Keita is an all-time great definitely. His achievement at club level is unmatched by any African midfielder ever. Keita consistently held on to a first-team spot in Pep Guardiola's Barca regarded as the best football team of all time. Keita won three La Liga titles, two Copa Del Reys, three Supercopa de Espana and two Champions League, two UEFA Super Cups and two Club World Cup titles during his time in Barcelona. He also won titles at Lorient and Sevilla and netted 78 goals from midfield.

660) **RABAH MADJER (ALGERIA)** - A pretty unfamiliar name to start this ranking with but "Mustapha" is an all-time great. Widely regarded as the best Algerian footballer ever and was named the outright best of the last century. He is a legend for Portuguese

outfit FC Porto as his goal was crucial in the 1987 European Cup final which he helped his side win. This was after he helped Algeria reach their first-ever World Cup finals in 1982. Madjer won nine major titles with Porto and scored more than 150 goals.

661) **ABEDI PELE (GHANA)** – Abedi Ayew, known professionally as Abedi Pele, is a Ghanaian former professional footballer who played as an attacking midfielder and who served as captain of the Ghana national team. He is regarded as one of the greatest African footballers of all time. He played for several European clubs and found his fame in the French Ligue 1 with Lille and Marseille, the latter where he won the UEFA Champions League in 1993, among other titles.

662) **HOSSAM HASSAN** - He is an Egyptian former professional football player who played as a striker. A prolific goalscorer, he is Egypt's all-time top scorer with 68 goals in 176 appearances. His twin brother Ibrahim also played professional football, and they shared teams for most of their extensive careers. Hassan represented the national team in the 1990 World Cup and seven Africa Cup of Nations tournaments. He is regarded as one of the best players in African football history and is the second-most capped player in men's international football.

663) **Mohamed Aboutrika** - is an Egyptian retired professional footballer who played as an attacking midfielder and a forward. He is often considered the best Egyptian player in history and is widely regarded as one of the greatest African footballers of all time. He also came second in the African Footballer of the Year award in 2008 after Emmanuel Adebayor and was one of five nominees for the 2006 award, and one of the ten nominated for the 2013 award. Aboutrika won the African Cup of Nations in 2006 with the Egyptian national team. He also scored the winning goal to help Egypt win the 2008 Africa Cup of Nations. He helped his club Al Ahly to win the bronze medal in the FIFA Club World Cup in 2006.

664) **Wael Gomaa** - is an Egyptian retired professional footballer who played as a centre-back. He is regarded as the best Egyptian centre-back ever and one of the best players in African football history.

665) **Samuel Osei Kuffour** is a Ghanaian retired professional footballer who played as a defender. Known for his great physical power, he is best remembered for his time with Bayern Munich, whom he represented for over a decade, winning a total of 14 honours, and playing in nearly 250 official matches. Kuffour appeared with the

Ghanaian national team in the 2006 World Cup, as well as five Africa Cup of Nations.

666) **Michael Kojo Essien** - is a Ghanaian former professional footballer who played as a midfielder. He was capped for the Ghana national team more than 50 times. Essien started his career playing for Liberty Professionals in Ghana. In 2000, he moved to France to join Bastia, where he would spend three seasons and appear in over 60 matches before joining Ligue 1 title holders Lyon in 2003. At Lyon, Essien won back-to-back league titles in 2003–04 and 2004–05 and won Ligue 1 Player of the Year in 2005. During his five-year stint in France, he acquired French citizenship. In 2005, Essien signed with Premier League side Chelsea for a £24.4 million transfer fee and, at the time of his signing, was the most expensive African footballer in history. At Chelsea, Essien helped the club win the Premier League in 2006 and 2010, as well as three FA Cups and one League Cup. He won the UEFA Champions League in 2012, while also placing as runner up in the 2008 UEFA Champions League. He has won the Chelsea Goal of the Season award twice, in the 2006–07 and 2008–09 seasons. Essien is a former Ghanaian international. At youth level, he represented his country at the 1999 FIFA U-17 World Championship and 2001 FIFA World Youth

Championship, with the latter team finishing as runner-up. Essien made his senior team debut in January 2002 and has represented his nation at three Africa Cup of Nations tournaments. Essien has also represented Ghana at the 2006 and 2014 FIFA World Cups.

667) **Thomas N'Kono** - is a Cameroonian former professional footballer. Arguably the greatest goalkeeper Africa ever produced; he was mainly associated with Espanyol, whom he represented for almost a decade playing more than 300 official matches. N'Kono appeared for the Cameroon national team in three World Cups, and four Africa Cup of Nations tournaments.

668) **Theophilus Khumalo -** also known as Doctor Khumalo, is a South African former soccer player. He is best known for being a star midfielder for Kaizer Chiefs as well as the South African national team.

669) **Geremi Sorele Njitap Fotso -** known simply as Geremi, is a Cameroonian former footballer. He was a versatile player able to play at right-back, right midfield or defensive midfielder, known for his power, combative style and free-kick ability. Geremi is often regarded as one of the greatest practitioners of the step over and often used it to fool his opponents before scoring one of his many goals. The most successful periods of Geremi's club career came at Real Madrid and Chelsea, winning

the UEFA Champions League with the first and domestic honours with the latter. Geremi earned 118 caps for Cameroon from 1996 to 2010, scoring 13 goals. He was a member of their squad for seven Africa Cup of Nations tournaments, winning in 2000 and 2002, as well as the World Cup in 2002 and 2010 and a gold medal at the 2000 Olympics.

670) **Patrick Pule "Ace" Ntsoelengoe OIS** - was a South African football player who is widely considered as one of the greatest the country has ever produced.

671) **Mohamed Barakat** - is a retired Egyptian footballer. A right-footed playmaker, Barakat usually played as an offensive right-winger or attacking midfielder for Egyptian club Al Ahly and the Egyptian National Team. He is considered by many as one of the most talented players in Africa. Barakat's hallmarks are surging runs from midfield which often disrupt opposing defences, as well as his box-to-box work ethic, which makes him an important figure both in defence and attack. Thanks to his noticeable achievements and talent, his fans have given him the nickname The Mercurial, He reached his peak in 2005 and 2006, helping his club Al Ahly to win the CAF Champions League 2005 and CAF Champions League 2006 and Egypt win their fifth African Cup of Nations

Egypt 2006. However, in 2006 his career was marred by a long spell of injuries.

672) **Mahmoud El-Khatib** - Nicknamed Bibo, El-Khatib was Egypt's icon during the 70s and 80s. He was honoured as African Footballer of the Year in 1983 and was also named as the Arab Sportsman of the 20th century. He was recognised by IFFHS as the joint 11th-best African player of the last century and by CAF in 2007 as the second greatest. El-Khatib won the continental crown with Egypt in 1986 and also played at the Olympic Games two years earlier. A hugely dominant figure with Al-Ahly, El-Khatib won almost a dozen domestic titles with the Cairene giants and also helped build the club's continental reputation, with their first two CAF Champions League triumphs in 1982 and 1987.

673) **Emad Moteab** - Egyptian forward Emad Moteab is not a player that typically belongs in such exalted company and among such illustrious names; however, a glance at the striker's goal record and big-game impact should convince that his record demands re-evaluation. He was named Africa's finest striker in 2005, the same year that he was top-scorer in the Egyptian Premier League.

674) **Bruce David Grobbelaar** - is a Zimbabwean former professional footballer who played as a goalkeeper, most

prominently for English team Liverpool between 1981 and 1994, and the Zimbabwean national team. He is remembered for his gymnastic-like athletic ability, unflappable confidence and eccentric and flamboyant style of play. He has been the goalkeeper coach for Ottawa Fury FC of the North American Soccer League since 2014. In March 2018 he was announced as goalkeeper coach for the Matabeleland football team.

675) **Laureano Bisan-Etame Mayer -** commonly known as Lauren, is a retired Cameroonian footballer of Equatoguinean origin who formerly played as a right-back for the Cameroonian national team. As an Arsenal player, he won several trophies and is known as one of the 'Invincibles', a title given to the Arsenal squad in 2004 after they went undefeated in the 2003–04 season and won the Premier League title. He also won an Olympic Gold Medal at the 2000 Sydney Olympics and two Africa Cup of Nations titles in 2000 and 2002 with Cameroon. He holds dual Cameroonian-Spanish nationality due to being raised in Spain.

676) **Ahmed Hassan -** One of the finest African passers of his generation, Hassan was a sprightly wide player earlier in his career before moving inside to dictate the play as age crept up on him. In both 2006 and 2010, he was the AFCON player of the tournament. He suffers, like his

teammates, for a persistent failure to qualify for the World Cup. A four-time Cup of Nations champion with Egypt, Hassan remains the world's most-capped male player ever. His 184 outings for the Pharaohs are unlikely to be bested anytime soon.

677) **Théophile Abega Mbida,** nicknamed Doctor, was a Cameroonian football player and politician. Playing as a midfielder he was part of the Cameroon national football team, playing all three matches at the 1982 FIFA World Cup and captaining the side to their first African Nations Cup victory in 1984, where he scored a goal in the final. He was nicknamed "The Doctor" in tribute to his footballing intelligence.

678) **Emmanuel Amuneke** - It is certainly true that Amuneke didn't have a career quite as glittering as his talent should have permitted, but the fact that the player's injury record associates him eternally tells its own story. Recognised by IFFHS as the joint 26th-best African player of the last century, this one-time African Footballer of the Year was once runner-up and a former BBC African Player of the Year. Not a bad haul for one so regularly stuck in the treatment room. Part of the glorious Nigerian generation of the 90s, Amuneke won Olympic gold and an African title in the early 90s as well as represented the Super Eagles at USA '94.

679) **Jean Manga-Onguene** - Recognised by IFFHS as the joint 34th-best African player of the last century, Manga-Onguene won the CAF Footballer of the Year award in 1980. Bad timing cost him the glory of his successors with the Cameroon national side. Manga-Onguene ceased his national team duty only three years before the Indomitable Lions' first African title. He returned to manage the national side during a brief, unsuccessful period in the late 90s.

680) **Benni McCarthy** - Don't let the flabby, ignominious end to his career distract you; Benni McCarthy was once one of Africa's most feared frontmen. Despite having never won a Cup of Nations with South Africa, McCarthy was the outstanding individual in the 1998 edition. He both was the top scorer and identified as the tournament's finest player. Represented Bafana Bafana at two World Cups, but he infamously missed out on home soil in 2010. He remains South Africa's top scorer of all time.

681) **Pat Mboma** - Mboma was an incredibly powerful individual with terrific technical prowess to match. He was African Footballer of the Year and BBC African Footballer of the Year in 2000. An incredibly consistent goalscorer for the Indomitable Lions, his numbers match up against almost all the other forwards on this list.

Mboma won the honours to go with his goals as well, as the figurehead in the great Cameroon side of the early 2000s. Alongside that excellent collection of stars, he won two AFCON titles, Olympic gold and featured at two World Cups. One of only six players to be top scorer at two different Cup of Nations tournaments.

682) **Salif Keita -** Named the African Footballer of the Year in 1970, Keita also received the FIFA Order of Merit in 1996. A lethal striker in his day, he enjoyed a stunning scoring record in France with Saint-Etienne. Keita guided Mali to the final of the 1972 Cup of Nations but was helpless as the Republic of Congo beat Les Aigles 3-2 in a classic final.

683) **Kazadi Mwamba -** The only one of the iconic Zaire side of the late 60s and early 70s to make this list, Kazadi was the goalkeeper of the 1974 World Cup that had its reputation so tainted by their failings in which their numbers almost impossible to dispute. Once a runner-up in the African Footballer of the Year award, Kazadi was recognised by IFFHS among the finest five African goalkeepers of the last century. Twice an African champion with Zaire in 1968 and 1974—the year of the Leopard's great voyage to the World Cup in West Germany—Mwamba was named Player of the Tournament following the 1968 triumph.

684) **Joseph-Antoine Bell** - Bell was recognised by IFFHS as Africa's greatest goalkeeper during the 20th century and was twice runner-up in the African Footballer of the Year award. Twice champion of Africa, Bell travelled with the Indomitable Lions on three World Cup sojourns.

685) **Rashidi Yekini** - Africa has produced a multitude of players who knew how to find the net with unflinching regularity; however, unlike Godfrey Chitalu and Tony Yeboah for example, Yekini has the honours to back up his tremendous work in front of goal. The Bull of Kaduna was once named African Footballer of the Year and has also come in in second and third place in the voting. He was recognised by IFFHS as the 17th-best African player of the last century. Part of the Nigerian team that conquered Africa in 1994, Yekini also starred at the World Cup in America later that year. He was the top scorer in two continental championships and was the player of the tournament in 1994.

686) **Karim Abdul Razak** - Golden Boy may not be a household name to most of you, but the Ghanaian midfielder with miraculous close control has an outstanding record that places him firmly within my top 50. A one-time African Footballer of the Year, he was recognised by IFFHS as the joint 31st-best African player of the last century. Razak was Player of the Tournament

in 1978 as he guided the Black Stars to their third African title.

687) **Tarek Dhiab -** This marvellous Tunisian playmaker was named Footballer of the Year in 1977 and was recognised by IFFHS as the joint 15th-best African player of the last century. He never managed to guide Tunisia to the AFCON title but did give the world a glimpse of his (and his compatriots') talents at the 1978 World Cup.

688) **Lucas Radebe -** Radebe was an elegant, consistent defender who led by example and enjoyed a storied career in South Africa and Yorkshire. Leeds United's Player of the Season in 1998, he could have achieved much more had he moved to Manchester United when Sir Alex Ferguson came calling in 2000. Radebe, who was once identified by Nelson Mandela as the great man's "hero," was one of the Nation Builders who won the Cup of Nations with South Africa in 1996. He also represented Bafana Bafana at two World Cups in 1998 and 2002.

689) **Daniel Amokachi -** Amokachi was recognised by IFFHS as the 18th-best African player of the last century. His failings at Everton, where he struggled to muscle his way past Duncan Ferguson and Paul Rideout, should not diminish his standing. Twice he came in third place in the

African Footballer of the Year Award. Amokachi played at the World Cups of 1994 and 1998 with Nigeria and was also a key member of the iconic Super Eagles side that triumphed at the AFCON in '94. He also won a historic Olympic gold in 1996, playing his part in a famous final victory over Argentina.

690) **Mahamadou Diarra** - Diarra was a tough-tackling midfielder who, along with Michael Essien, forged the basis of that excellent Lyon side that so often threatened to take the French side to the next level during the middle of the last decade. The Mali captain guided the team to third place at the Under-20 World Cup in 1999 but has struggled to win anything with Les Eigles over the last decade. The side is already eliminated from the running for next summer's World Cup. Diarra's place on this list is all about his domestic form last decade. Between 2002 and 2008 he won the league title, be it in France or Spain (with Real Madrid) every season—six consecutive major titles, not to mention a swathe of domestic cups.

691) **Rigobert Song** - A wild boy earlier in his career, Tonton has gently emerged as the wise old head of Cameroonian football—becoming an African icon in the process. Song remains, along with Zinedine Zidane, the only player to be sent off at two World Cups. A two-time AFCON winner, Song was the tournament's star man in

2002 as the Indomitable Lions retained their continental crown. He has represented the central African giants at a remarkable four World Cups—the most of any player on this list.

692) **Rachid Mekhloufi** - A big-game player and key influence in numerous important clashes, the forward was one of the first (and most visible) African-born players to represent the French national side. He remains the second-highest scorer in the history of AS Saint-Etienne. Mekhloufi failed to win much with the Desert Lions, with his greatest contribution came as part of the Front de Liberation Nationale side that travelled the world representing their countrymen then under French rule. The FLN team became one of Africa's most potent symbols of national identity and autonomy. He represented France four times, but also played at the 1982 World Cup with Algeria.

693) **Victor Ikpeba** - Ikpeba was recognised by IFFHS as the joint-34th-best African player of the last century. He was named African Footballer of the Year in 1997 and won the Ebony Shoe as the finest African player in the Belgian league in 1993. A continental champion with Nigeria in 1994, Ikpeba was also part of the team that won the Olympic gold two years later. He represented Nigeria at two World Cups. A Ligue 1 champion with

Monaco in 1997 and a Belgian Cup winner with RFC Liege in 1990, Ikpeba also enjoyed a stint with Borussia Dortmund.

694) **Noureddine Naybet** - Surely one of the finest—and certainly one of the most consistent—defenders Africa has ever produced, Naybet was a stalwart for Morocco and also made a successful transition to European football. He was another great African defender linked with Manchester United. Naybet represented the Atlas Lions in two World Cups, but, like Mustapha Hadji, remained unfulfilled at the Cup of Nations. He won the African Champions League with Wydad Casablanca in 1992, a triumph which earned him a move across the Mediterranean. He won the Spanish championship with Deportivo La Coruna in 2000, before further supplementing his trophy haul with several Spanish Cups.

695) **Segun Odegbami** - "Mathematical" made the podium for African Footballer of the Year in both 1977 and 1980 without ever having won the big one. Odegbami was recognised by IFFHS as the joint-19th best African player of the last century. Odegbami guided Nigeria to their maiden African title, on home soil, in 1980. He was twice top scorer in the Cup of Nations, in 1978 and 1980,

and remains Nigeria's second-highest scorer of all time, behind only the peerless Rashidi Yekini.

696) **Kolo Toure** - Another of Cote d'Ivoire's famed Golden Generation, the elder Toure is an athletic, imposing centre-back who has had his fair share of controversy and mishap. Toure suffered the misfortune of his countrymen as the recent incarnation of the Elephants so often stumbled at the business end of the Cup of Nations. He has represented his nation at two World Cups.

697) **Laurent Pokou** - Second-place African Footballer of the Year in 1970 and third-place three years later, Pokou was a big-game player and is considered one of the continent's finest forwards. An excellent dribbler and a terrifically efficient finisher. Pele once identified Pokou as his successor. Pele. I would argue that only Rashidi Yekini and Roger Milla have made an individual impact at the Cup of Nations comparable to that of Pokou. The Ivorian was top scorer twice—in 1968 and 1970—and was also the Player of the Tournament in the latter competition.

698) **Finidi George** - Named by the International Federation of Football History and as the 10th-best African player of the last century, George was a sinuous winger who, at least during the early part of his career,

was a direct and menacing threat from the flanks. Considered among the finest wingers in the world during the early 90s…but not so much during his failed stint in England with Ipswich. George represented Nigeria at the 1994 and 1998 World Cups and was also part of the Super Eagles' irrepressible 1994 AFCON-winning side. He made a subsequent three continental semi-finals with Nigeria. George was finely furnished with honours at Ajax where, alongside countryman Kanu, he won the Champions League in 1995 and lost a final in 1996. Also picked up three Dutch League titles, a UEFA Super Cup, an Intercontinental Cup and two Dutch Supercups.

699) **Marc-Vivien Foe** - The cornerstone of the Cameroonian side that so dazzled at the turn of the millennium, the defensive midfielder's life was cut short during the Confederations Cup as he suffered heart failure. Foe won two continental crowns with Cameroon—in 2000 and 2002—and also represented the side at the 1994 and 2002 World Cups. He would have been present in 1998 as well but missed the tournament due to injury. A French league champion with both Lens and Lyon, he also won a couple of French League Cups and a Cameroonian Cup with Canon Yaounde.

700) **Mustapha Hadji** - Hadji was an agile, innovative, imaginative attacking midfielder who excelled with the

ball at his feet and defence ahead of him. He was named African Footballer of the Year in 1998—the only non-West African to win the award in over two decades. He qualified for two World Cups with the Moroccan side and impressed at France in 1998. His showing against Norway remains one of the finest performances by an African player on the global stage. The Atlas Lions never quite flourished in continental competition during this time though and Hadji never won the African Nations Cup.

Source

- https://www.blackhistorymonth.org.uk/article/section/history-of-slavery/africa-before-transatlantic-enslavement/
- https://mg.co.za/article/2015-03-12-13-facts-about-slavery-in-africa/
- https://blackhistorystudies.com/resources/resources/100-things-about-africa/
- https://theconversation.com/american-slavery-separating-fact-from-myth-79620
- https://www.britannica.com/topic/transatlantic-slave-trade
- https://africa-facts.org/african-culture-16-most-interesting-traditions/
- https://www.africantrails.co.uk/tour-info/africa-culture-and-history/
- https://www.southwales.ac.uk/story/3054/
- https://blog.rhinoafrica.com/2018/08/13/7-amazing-african-tribal-traditions/
- https://www.history.com/news/7-influential-african-empires
- https://www.astepintonature.com/2018/09/05/10-mind-blowing-facts-about-africa/

- http://emeagwali.com/media/africa/100-greatest-africans-of-all-times.html
- https://www.history.com/news/8-black-inventors-african-american
- https://en.wikipedia.org/
- https://www.aljazeera.com/news/2018/2/20/mapping-africas-natural-resources
- https://www.bbc.co.uk/news/world-africa-54158901
- https://en.wikipedia.org/wiki/List_of_World_Heritage_Sites_in_Africa
- http://whc.unesco.org/en/list/
- https://soccernet.ng/2019/02/top-10-greatest-african-players-of-all-time.html
- https://www.coolaboo.com/world-history/ancient-africa/the-greatest-kings-of-ancient-africa
- https://thegrio.com/2015/06/21/great-african-kings/
- https://www.independent.co.uk/news/world/africa/art-of-africa-the-50-best-african-artists-426441.html
- https://afktravel.com/71524/15-greatest-african-empires/16/
- https://news.harvard.edu/gazette/story/2015/10/the-spirituality-of-africa/
- https://blog.oup.com/2014/05/15-facts-on-african-religions/
- https://blackhistorystudies.com/

- https://theconversation.com/colonialism-was-a-disaster-and-the-facts-prove-it-84496
- https://www.britannica.com/place/western-Africa/Colonization
- https://hikebiketravel.com/
- https://fee.org/
- https://www.factretriever.com/

Printed in Dunstable, United Kingdom

73912242R00117